BALANCE IN TEACHING

[XI]

FOUNDATIONS OF WALDORF EDUCATION

RUDOLF STEINER

Balance in Teaching

STUTTGART
September 15-22, 1920 and October 15-16, 1923

& Anthroposophic Press

*The publisher wishes to acknowledge the inspiration
and support of Connie and Robert Dulaney*

* * *

Copyright © SteinerBooks, 2007

Published by Anthroposophic Press/SteinerBooks
610 Main Street, Great Barrington, MA 01230
www.steinerbooks.org

This book is volume 302a in the Collected Works of Rudolf Steiner. It is a translation of *Erziehung und Unterricht aus Menschenerkenntnis*, published by Rudolf Steiner Verlag, Dornach, Switzerland. Part I: "Balance in Teaching" is a revised translation by Ruth Pusch © Mercury Press, 1982, used with permission of Mercury Press, Spring Valley, NY. Part II: "Deeper Insights into Education" is translated by René Querido © Anthroposophic Press, 1983.

Library of Congress Cataloging-in-Publication Data is available.

CONTENTS

LECTURE TWO

Forces Leading to Health and Illness in Education

Why do we educate? Education is a metamorphosis of the healing process as humans unfold their being on Earth. Teachers must learn to regard things in their educational application as either bringing health or being injurious to health, rather than being "true" or "false." Understanding the principle of healing through knowledge of our relation to the world around us. True feelings of enthusiasm and responsibility must arise in teachers.

LECTURE THREE

A Comprehensive Knowledge of the Human Being as the Source of Imagination in the Teacher

A description of the processes of health and illness continually taking place in the human organism. Everything one does affects these processes. Teachers are coworkers in the actual guidance of the world. What is needed to adopt the right attitude toward the task of true education: example of Mahatma Gandhi. Teachers must unite themselves with the archangel Michael to work for the healing of humanity.

INTRODUCTION

by Douglas Gerwin

HIGH up in the wooded mountains of Phokis stands a circle
of tall fluted columns marking the secluded temple of Delphi.
According to legend, Zeus released two eagles from opposite
ends of the world, and the craggy olive grove where these two
mighty messengers converged he designated as being the *Ompha-
lus*, the navel of the world. Eventually this meeting place became
the sacred precinct for two Greek deities, who occupied a temple
erected on this quiet mountainside. It was said that Apollo and
Dionysus took up residence at Delphi during each year; first
Apollo and then Dionysus, but never both at the same time.

These two gods—Apollo and Dionysus—embody polar
complementary forces that work in opposite ways to develop the
child and young adult, but they also help teachers educate children to grow into strong and, above all, healthy human beings.
Rudolf Steiner describes how children first come into the world
primarily under the radiant formative guidance of Apollo; but
already in the early years, and certainly by the second dentition,
the turbulent stirrings of Dionysus begin to arise in these increas-
ingly independent young human beings. The central task of teachers is to permit these alternating forces to play themselves out in
the developing children and adolescents without overwhelming
them. How to do this?

This question stands at the heart of two series of lectures that Rudolf Steiner held towards the end of his life in Stuttgart, Germany, for teachers at the original Waldorf school. The first set was given as follow-up to an intense two-week teacher education course that Steiner had offered these teachers just before the school opened in 1919.[1] In a series of four lectures given a year later, in September 1920, Steiner described the polar opposite forces that work on the developing child and spelled out in rare detail how teachers could use the curriculum to balance these forces. The second set, held just over three years later, in October of 1923, focused more on the historically changing mission of the teacher—from Greek gymnast and Roman rhetorician to modern professor—and laid out the need for teachers to collaborate more intimately with the medical profession in the healthy unfolding of youth.

In both lecture series (herein collected for the first time in English as a single volume), Steiner explores the effects on the child of what he variously calls, on the one hand, sculptural or etheric formative forces and, on the other, musical or astral forces. These formative forces, like a sculptor taking hold of a handful of clay, work in the spirit of Apollo from the whole to the part. They act with a centripetal gesture—starting from the vast expanses of the periphery—to form and ground and center a child: in short, to incarnate the child into unique flesh and bone, distinct blood and nerve. The other forces, like a musician taking up a trumpet or drum, work in the spirit of Dionysus from individual elements to the whole. They act with a centrifugal gesture—starting with distinct parts, like individual notes—to build and expand and extend a child: in short, to excarnate it from the confines of the

---

1. In English, this course is available in three separate volumes: *Study of Man* (published also as *Foundations of Human Experience*), *Discussions with Teachers*, and *Practical Advice to Teachers*.

physical world and connect it with the whole periphery of the spiritual world.

Left to themselves, these forces can work one-sidedly on the growing child, with devastating consequences. Allow the sculptural, formative, centripetal, linear forces of Apollo to exert too strong a grip, and we can see children grow prematurely stiff in carriage and sometimes burdened of soul, like grumpy little gnomes trapped in the confines of precociously sclerotic bodies. Allow the musical, centrifugal, curvilinear forces of Dionysus to rise up too strongly, and we can see children who stay youthful and carefree too long, like flighty Peter Pans or fluid slender sylphs. Here Rudolf Steiner offers exceptionally specific suggestions on how teachers can use the subjects of the curriculum—both academic and artistic— either as parachutes to buoy a child's overly precipitous descent into the physical body, or as anchors or tethers to coax a reluctant being down into corporeal existence on earth. Even the same subject matter, he shows, can be used to one purpose or the other, depending upon what the child or adolescent is asked to do with it. Children overly prone to becoming trapped in the body need to draw, write, and revel in the details of a subject in order to loosen their "I" a little from the confines of the physical organism. By contrast, children who have difficulty taking hold of the physical organism need to *observe*, as from a bird's eye view, what they have drawn or written, or be encouraged to attend to the overall *meaning* or *context* of a subject, rather than its details.

Underlying these suggestions is the general maxim: Move, and you excarnate; be still, and you incarnate. But the *result* of movement is that you feel more incarnated, as for instance after a brisk walk; of being still, that you feel more buoyant and excarnated, as for instance after a period of silent contemplation. As in any organic polarity, opposite forces such as movement and stasis, far from canceling the effects of each other, actually help to *generate* them.

In other words, the forces of stilling and moving represent two vital principles of human development. The sculptural forces represented by the archetype of Apollo serve to induce calm, stability, and ultimately quiescence, even to the point of rigidity. What Steiner calls musical forces, represented by the archetype of Dionysus, serve to stir activity, instability, and ultimately dynamic motion, even to the point of dissolution. In Greek mythology the first was called *Kosmos* ("form coming to rest"), the second *Kaos* ("restless void").

These complementary principles—movement and stasis—can be found in two bodily systems by which most of our classroom learning proceeds: the auditory and the visual systems. Ear and larynx, connected by the Eustachian tube, form a single sensory system, as anyone knows who has watched small children subtly mouth the words they are hearing. In his study of the human senses, Rudolf Steiner maintains that even in order to *hear* the spoken word in a conversation we have actually to reproduce gently the living etheric *movements* of the larynx that formed it.[2] Indeed, we hear something only when it moves, and we hear only when the ear itself vibrates. In other words, our sense of hearing is profoundly integrated into the world of movement.[3]

---

2. See Rudolf Steiner's lecture (Stuttgart, December 9, 1922) on "The Ear" published in the annual journal *The Golden Blade 1970*, ed. Adam Bittleston, p. 24.

3. See Armin Husemann, *The Harmony of the Human Body: Musical Principles in Human Physiology* (Edinburgh: Floris Books, 1994). Husemann, a celebrated school doctor and accomplished pianist, opened his lecture series at the 2002 Kolisko Conference of Waldorf teachers and therapists in Lahti, Finland, with the question: "What happens if someone tells you a joke while you and your friends are lifting a heavy grand piano?" His answer—that you are unable to laugh unless you first set the piano down on the floor— graphically illustrated how deeply the larynx is embedded in our musculatory system. Hoist a piano off the ground and we stretch taut every muscle of our body, including the muscles of the larynx; once stretched, these laryngeal muscles prevent us from laughing.

This system of ear and larynx, so utterly reliant upon our ability to move and be moved, stands in polar contrast to another sensory system which depends on our ability to slow down movement almost (though never entirely) to the point of complete quiet. This is the pictorial or visual sense given to us through our eyes. While each eye is surrounded by six (some say seven) muscles that allow us to roll our eyeballs, squint at a distant object, or simply stare at something close to hand, we see only when our eyes—and the head in which they are set—come to a fleeting moment of focus and rest.

These two sensory systems, and their reciprocal roles in our development as in the processes of perceiving and remembering, Rudolf Steiner explores in bold and sometimes convoluted ways. For instance, he suggests that eye and ear both perceive and remember in radically opposite ways. We have a dim sense of this if we notice how very different is the experience of a picture remembered from a tune remembered. Any advertiser knows is it easier to lodge a catchy melody in the mind than a pretty picture. A visual image may need to be exceptionally shocking or clever to stick in our thoughts, but even the most trivial musical jingle can get caught up in the revolving door of the mind. Why is this?

Rudolf Steiner explains that we perceive or take in pictorial impressions with the visual (and other) senses of our nervous system, centered in the brain, but we comprehend these impressions only to the degree that they sink down to be worked upon by our rhythmic systems of respiration and circulation; furthermore, he says, we commit them to lasting memory only if we fully digest them by means of our powers of metabolism and will as expressed through our limbs.

With aural impressions, according to Steiner, the sequence is reversed. Sounds we perceive or take in via our will—through metabolism and limbs. Whereas we tend to stand still when we look—for instance at a painting in a museum gallery or at the sweep of a valley from a mountaintop vista—we are much more likely to move to what we hear, especially if the sound is musical. In other words, we perceive sound with our full body, not just with our ears. These impressions must be lifted into our systems of circulation and breathing, the semi-consciousness of heart and lung, if they are to be comprehended, and only then can these auditory perceptions rise up into the brain and nervous system, where they are livingly remembered. "In the same regions where we perceive the visible [i.e. the brain], we remember the audible. In the same regions where we remember the visible [i.e. the limbs], we perceive the audible. And the two cross over each other like a lemniscate in the rhythmic system" (page 35). To the degree that we become conscious of this crossing over, he adds, we can "hear colors" and "see sounds." This description casts entirely new light on the learning habits of so-called "visual learners" and "auditory learners"; the one is learning top down, so to speak; the other, bottom up.

Complicating, and perhaps confusing, this schema is the notion that the workings of eye and ear—and the forces they embody—change dramatically as we grow from infant to young adult. On the one hand, even with the embryo, we can see that physically we grow *down* from head to toes under the influence of powerfully formative, "sculptural" forces. These, according to Steiner, radiate from the head, especially during the pre-school years, giving shape to the child's developing body. Apollo inhabits the human temple first. On the other hand, and harder to recognize, is a countervailing stream of "musical" forces which, starting from the sixth or seventh year, begin to challenge these sculptural forces, resulting in the developmental milestones of the second dentition, the so-called "nine-year-old change," and the voice shift at puberty. Around the onset of adolescence this collision of opposite forces is further complicated by what Steiner calls a battle between inner forces—both musical and sculptural—

threatening to break out and similarly named outer forces threatening to break in.

However we understand these sculptural and musical forces, it falls to the teachers to form their lessons in such a way that the children overcome their natural one-sidedness, for in overcoming imbalance they can achieve, or sustain, a condition of physical and emotional health. Only our rhythmic systems—of breath and blood, of lung and heart—are of themselves health giving, since in these the relationship of movement and stasis is more in equipoise. Here the collaboration between teacher and physician can be especially useful to further the child's healthy growth and development, for the doctor engages at the unconscious level just those therapeutic forces that the teacher employs at the conscious level. "The forces inherent in education are metamorphoses of therapeutic forces" (page 88). In a sense, education begins where medicine leaves off.

This brings us to a consideration of education as a health-bearing endeavor. All too easily teachers can set their mission according to what is right and what is wrong in their students and, for that matter, with their colleagues. Students are assessed in terms of results viewed as correct or incorrect; colleagues in terms of deeds judged as being wrong or right. While these forms of evaluation have their place, Rudolf Steiner is at pains to describe how these terms lose their meaning and their value when education shifts from physical to metaphysical realities. "As soon as we reach the spiritual world we must substitute 'healthy' and 'ill' for 'true' and 'false.'. . . In the physical world things can be 'right'; in the spiritual world nothing is 'wrong' or 'right'" (pages 88-89). To the degree that education involves spiritual processes, then, teachers need to evaluate their lessons not just on the merit of their correctness but also on the degree to which they create health. "We must learn to regard things in their educational application as either healthy or unhealthy, injurious to health.

This is of particular significance if one wishes to engender a true consciousness of oneself as a teacher" (page 89).

In this context, it may help to recall the verse Rudolf Steiner gave to young physicians as part of their training with him. More recently this verse is spoken each morning during the Kolisko conferences held every four years for educators and therapists:

> Powerfully there lived in ancient times
> Among the souls of the Initiates the thought
> That every person coming into the world
> Is ill by nature;
> Education was then seen as a healing process,
> Bringing to the child, as it matured,
> The health it needed
> To become a full human being.[4]

* * * * * *

A final note on reading this text: The first lecture series of this volume, previously published in English as *Balance in Teaching*, appeared in German under the title, supposedly suggested by Marie Steiner, of *Meditativ erarbeitete Menschenkunde*—literally "the study of the human being worked on meditatively." The second set of lectures in this book, originally issued in English under the title *Deeper Insights into Education: The Waldorf School Approach*, has also been published separately in German as *Anregungen zur innerlichen Durchdringung des Lehr- und Erzieherberufes*—literally "suggestions concerning the inner penetration of the teachers' and

---

4. Rudolf Steiner's verse to young doctors. See, for instance, Michaela Glöckler et al, *Education—Health for Life: Education and Medicine Working Together for Healthy Development*, Conference Companion to Kolisko Conferences 2006 (Dornach: School for Spiritual Science, 2006), p.9. Verse retranslated by Douglas Gerwin.

educators' profession." At least the German titles suggest that, notwithstanding his detailed suggestions, Steiner never intended these series as prescriptions for teaching but rather, like so many of his lectures, as indications for contemplative study and meditation. Especially his comments on ear and eye, on musical and sculptural forces, call for a contemplative rather than expository reading. Like the teacher who at the end of school exclaims, "How much have I learned this year!" we can profit from this compact set of lectures as much in light of our lessons as in preparing them.

Douglas Gerwin, Ph.D., is Director of the Center for Anthroposophy, including Chair of its Waldorf High School Teacher Education Program, and Co-Director of the Research Institute for Waldorf Education. Himself a Waldorf graduate, Dr. Gerwin has taught for over 25 years at university and high school levels in subjects ranging from biology and history to German and music. He is editor of four books related to Waldorf education—*For the Love of Literature: A Celebration of Language and Imagination* (published by Anthroposophic Press); *Genesis of a Waldorf High School; The Andover Proceedings: Tapping the Wellsprings of Health in Adolescence; And Who Shall Teach the Teachers: The Christ Impulse in Waldorf Education*—as well as author of various articles on adolescence and the Waldorf curriculum. This year he co-authored the *Survey of Waldorf Graduates*, the first comprehensive look at how North AmericanWaldorf graduates fare in college and beyond. He currently resides in Amherst, Massachusetts, with his wife Connie, a Waldorf high school teacher of math at the Hartsbrook School.

PART ONE

Balance In Teaching

1

The Educational Task of Central Europe

STUTTGART — SEPTEMBER 15, 1923

MY dear friends, during the days I am to spend here I had intended to give a kind of supplement to last year's introductory education course. But the days are so few and, after what I have just been told, there are so many things to be done that I can hardly say whether it will be possible to get beyond these scanty introductory words. It is almost impossible to speak of any kind of program.

I should like first to add to what I said to you last year about the teacher, the educator. Of course, all I shall say about the teacher's intrinsic being must be understood in a completely aphoristic way, and it will really be best if it gradually takes its true form within you yourselves, developing further through your own thinking and feeling. The College of Teachers must become aware that teachers especially must have a deep feeling for the nature of the esoteric. And in calling your attention to this, I will remind you that we base our work on anthroposophical spiritual science; in our school this spiritual science will shape the form of education necessary for our time. In this age of democracy and journalism, it seems that people hardly have a true or valid feeling for what is meant by "esoteric." We sometimes believe that what is true is true, what is right is right, and the true and the right can be proclaimed before the world, once they are formulated in a way one considers correct. But in real life this is not the case; things are quite different. In real life the essential point is that you can unfold a certain kind of effectiveness in your actions only if the impulse for this effectiveness is guarded in the soul as a most sacred, secret possession. Teachers in particular must guard many things as sacred, secret possessions, and must look upon these as something that only play a part in those meetings and discussions carried on within the College of Teachers itself. At first a statement of this kind does not seem particularly clear, and yet it will become so. I could say a good deal more, but it will begin to be understandable if I say that the principle I have just stated has universal significance for the present age, embracing the entire civilization of our time.

When we think about the education of the young today, we must bear in mind that we are concerned with the feelings, ideas, and will impulses of the next generation; we must be clear that our present task is to prepare this next generation for definite tasks that must be accomplished some time in humanity's future. When this is said, the question at once arises: Why is it then that humanity has reached its present condition of widespread misery? Humanity has arrived at this misery because it has, in essential things, really made itself dependent—through and through dependent—on the kind of thinking and feeling peculiar to the West. When someone in Central Europe—someone involved in external public life, a journalist, best-selling author, or the like—speaks today in Berlin or Vienna about Fichte, Herder, or even Goethe, they are further removed from the spiritual impulse living in these great men than they are from what is felt and thought today in London, Paris, New York, or Chicago. Things have gradually developed in such a way that in general our whole civilization has been flooded by the impulses proceeding from the philosophy of the Western nations. Our whole public life is permeated by their philosophy.

This is particularly true of the art of education. From the last third of the nineteenth century, European nations, generally speaking, have learned from the West in all these matters; today those who discuss or dispute questions of education take for granted that they should make use of the habits of Western thought. If you trace back all the educational ideas that are considered reasonable in Central Europe today, you will find their source in the views of Herbert Spencer[1] or personalities like him. People do not trace out the numerous paths by which the views of Spencer and the others have entered the heads of those who set the tone in cultural and spiritual questions in Central Europe, but these paths exist; they can be found. If you take the spirit of the educational thinking (never mind the details) such as is found in Fichte, it is not only absolutely different from what is generally considered sensible pedagogy today; modern people are actually hardly capable of bringing their souls into the direction of thinking and feeling needed to conceive how the intentions of Fichte and Herder can be developed further. Thus, we experience in education—especially in the art of education—that what has become the rule is exactly the opposite of what it should be. Let me point out to you what Spencer has written.

Spencer was of the opinion that pictorial instruction and object lessons in school should lead in later years to the experiments of the naturalist or into the research of the scientist. What then would have to be done in school? According to him, we should teach children in such a way that when they are grown up and have the opportunity, they can carry on what they have learned in school about minerals, plants, animals, and so on, so that they become proper scientific thinkers. It is true that this kind of idea is frequently opposed, but at the same time people really put this

---

1. Herbert Spencer (1820-1903), English philosopher.

principle into practice, simply because our textbooks are put together with this in mind, and no one would think of altering or doing away with our textbooks. Our botany textbooks today are written more for future botanists than for human beings in general. In the same way, zoology textbooks are not written for everyone, but for future zoologists.

Now the remarkable thing is that we ought to strive for the exact opposite of what Spencer laid down as a true educational principle. When we are teaching children about plants and animals in our elementary schools, we could hardly imagine a greater mistake in our educational method than to treat the subject as an introduction to studies required to become a botanist or zoologist. If, on the contrary, you plan your lessons so that your way of teaching about plants and animals hinders the children from becoming botanists or zoologists, you will have acted more wisely than by following Spencer's principle; for no one should become a botanist or zoologist through what he or she learns in the early grades. People become scientists only through their particular talents, revealed by their choice of vocation, which are certain to appear at maturity if there is a true art of education. Through their gifts! That is, if one has the gifts necessary for a botanist, one can become a botanist, and if one has the gifts necessary for a zoologist, one can become a zoologist. This can result only from the gifts of the children in question, which is to say, through predetermined karma. This must come about by our recognizing that one child has the makings of a botanist and another the makings of a zoologist. It must never be the result of forming our elementary school lessons in any way as a preparation for special scientific activity. Just think what has been happening. Our scientists, sad to say, have been taking on the field of pedagogy; people who have trained themselves to think scientifically have been engaging in education, have taken a most important part in deciding educational questions. The opinion is that the teacher as such has something in common with the scientist; a scientific training has actually been accepted as valid educational training, whereas the two should be completely and absolutely different. If the teacher is a scientist, and makes it his or her business in a limited sense to think scientifically (that one can do as a private person, but not as a teacher), quite often something happens. The teacher will cut a rather comical figure in the classroom and among the students or colleagues; jokes will be made at his or her expense. Goethe's "Baccalaureus"[2] in the upper classes is not such a rarity as is usually supposed.

Today if we were to ask whether we would side with the teachers when the students make jokes about them or uphold the students, we would in the present state of affairs in education side more with the students. The direction things have taken can be best observed in our universities. What are the universities, actually? Are they institutions for teaching young men and women or are they research centers? They would like to be both, and that is why they have become the exaggerations they are today. People even find it an excellent feature of our universities that they are at one and the same time institutions for teaching and for research. But this is just how all the muddle comes into education—it is carried out by scientists, works its way into our highest educational centers, later finds its way down into the high schools, and finally into the elementary schools.

However, it cannot be sufficiently borne in mind that the art of education must proceed from life itself and not from abstract scientific thought. It is peculiar that we have an educational methodology with a wholly scientific direction, while quite forgotten is what can be found in Herder, in Fichte, in Jean-Paul, in Schiller, and other great individuals, reminding us that there is really a

---

2. *Faust*, Part 2, Act 2. A student highly scornful of all his professors.

way of educating drawn directly from life, that is a life-infused education.

It is, moreover, the world-historical mission of the Central European peoples to cherish and develop this way of educating, to make it their esoteric task to develop it. There is much that will be possible for all humankind to do, working together; this must happen if improvement in the social sphere is to come about in the future. But what is emerging as an art of education from the whole of the spiritual culture that is specifically Central European, the peoples of the West will not be able to understand. In fact, it will annoy them. We can only speak to them about the art of education when they have made up their minds to discover and understand the esoteric foundation of spiritual science. All those things people in Germany have looked at with such pride over the last forty years, those things that have been considered such major advances, are of no possible use to Germany itself; they will just pass over into the dominion of the Western nations. There is nothing to be done about it. We can only hope to awaken so much understanding for the threefolding of the social organism that the Western nations will take part in it.

However, we do have something to give the world from Central Europe in respect to the art of education that no one else can give, neither an Eastern nor a Western person. But we must have the discretion to keep this in those circles that are able to understand it; we must understand how to guard it with a certain sense of trust, knowing that it is this guardianship that will make our work effective. You must know what things to be silent about in the presence of certain people if you want to obtain a result. Above all, we must be clear that there is nothing to hope for from the kind of thought coming to us from the West, which is indeed indispensable in many other branches of modern civilization. We must know that there is absolutely nothing to hope for from that quarter for the art of education we have to develop.

Herbert Spencer has written something of unusual interest about education. He has compiled a list of axioms, or "principles" as he calls them, about children's intellectual education. Among these is one on which he lays great emphasis: in teaching, one should never proceed from the abstract but always from the concrete; one should always elaborate a subject from an individual case. So he writes in his book on education, and there we find, before he enters into anything concrete, the worst thickets of abstraction, really nothing but abstract straw, and he does not notice that he himself is carrying out the opposite of just those principles he has argued are indispensable. We have here the example of an eminent and leading contemporary philosopher completely contradicting what he has just advocated.

You heard last year that our education is not to be built on abstract principles, or on one thing or another that someone says about "not bringing things to the child from outside but developing the child's individuality," and so on. You know that our educational art should be built upon a real sympathy with the child's nature, that it should be built up in the widest sense on knowledge of the growing child. In our first course of lectures and then later in our faculty meetings, we have actually brought together everything we need to know about the nature of the growing child. If as teachers we can enter into the child's unfolding, out of this understanding will arise the insight into how we need to act. In this respect, as teachers we must become artists. Just as it is impossible for an artist to pick up a book on aesthetics and then paint or carve according to the principles the writer has laid down, it should also be quite impossible for a teacher to use an "educational guide" in order to teach. What the teacher *does* need is insight into what the child really is and is becoming step by step through the stages of childhood. Above all we should be clear about the following. Say we teach, beginning with first grade, the six-year-olds. Every time we take a first grade, our teaching will be bad and will have failed to fulfill its purpose if, after working with this first grade for a year, we do not say to ourselves, "Who is it now who has really learned the most? It is I, the teacher!" But if we say to ourselves, "At the beginning of this school year I had excellent educational principles, I have followed the best teaching authorities, and have done everything to carry out these principles," if you really had done this, you most certainly would have taught badly. You would have taught best of all if each morning you had gone into your class in fear and trembling, without very much confidence in yourself, and then declared at the end of the year: I myself have really learned the most during this year! For your ability to say this depends on your actions; it depends on what you have really done, depends upon your constantly having had the feeling that you are growing while you are helping the children to grow, the feeling that you are experimenting in the highest sense of the word, that you are not really able to do so very much, but by working with the children there grows in you a certain strong capacity. Sometimes you will have the feeling that there is not much to be done with this or that kind of child, but you will have taken trouble with them. From other children, owing to their special gifts, you will have acquired a certain experience. In short, you leave the endeavor quite a different person than you were when you began, and you have learned to do what you were incapable of doing when you began to teach a year earlier. At the end of the school year you say yes, only now can I do what I ought to have been doing. This is a very real feeling! And hiding within it is a certain secret. If at the beginning of the school year you had really been able to do all you could do at the end, you would have taught badly. You gave good lessons because you had to work them out as you went along! I must put this in the form of a paradox. You taught well when you did not know at the beginning what you had then learned by the end of the year, and it would have been harmful if you had already known at the beginning of the year what you had learned by the end. A remarkable paradox!

It is important for many people to know this, but it is most important of all for teachers to know it. For this is a special instance of a general truth and insight: no matter what the subject is, a knowledge that can be comprehended in abstract principles, that can be represented by ideas in the mind, is of no practical value. Only what leads to this knowledge, what is found on the way to this knowledge is of practical value. The kind of knowledge that is ours after we have taught for a year first receives its value after our death. It is not until after death that this knowledge rises into such a reality that it can shape our development, that it can develop the individuality further. In life it is not the ready-made knowledge that has value, but the work that leads to this knowledge, and particularly in the art of education this work has its own special value. It is the same in education as in the arts. I cannot consider anyone an artist with the correct attitude who does not inwardly acknowledge upon finishing a piece of work: only now can I really do it. I do not think artists have the right attitude if they are satisfied with any work they have done. They may have a certain natural, egoistic respect for their work, but they cannot really be satisfied with it. In fact, a completed artwork loses a large part of its interest for the artist, and this loss of interest is due to the particular nature of the knowledge we are gaining while we make something. On the other hand, the living quality in a work of art, the life that springs from it, originates in the fact that it has not yet been transmuted into knowledge.

It is the same with the whole organism. Our head is as "finished" as anything can be finished, for it is formed out of the forces of our last incarnation; it is "overripe." All human heads are overripe, even the unripe ones—but the rest of the organism is only at the stage of furnishing the seed for the head in our next incarnation; it is full of life and growth, but it is incomplete. Not until our death will the rest of our organization really show its true form, namely, the form of the forces that are at work in it. The constitution of the rest of our organism shows that there is flowing life in it; ossification is reduced here to the minimum, while in our head it reaches the maximum.

A specific kind of inward humility, the sense that we ourselves are still only becoming, is something that will give teachers strength, for more arises out of this feeling than out of any abstract principles. If we stand in our classroom conscious that it is a good thing that we do everything imperfectly—for in that way there is life in what we do—we will teach well. If on the other hand we are always patting ourselves on the back over the perfection of our teaching, then it is quite certain we shall teach badly.

But now consider that you have been responsible for teaching the first grade, second grade, and so on, that you have gone through everything that has to be gone through, excitements, disappointments, successes, too, if you will. Consider that you have gone through all the classes of the elementary school; at the end of each year you have spoken to yourself somehow in the spirit I have just described, and now you make your way back down again from the eighth to the first grade. Well, now it might be supposed that you can say to yourself: Now I am beginning with what I have learned; now I shall be able to do it right; I shall be an excellent teacher! But it won't be like that. Experience will bring you inwardly to something quite different. At the end of the second, the third, and each subsequent school year, you will say exactly the same thing out of a right feeling: I have now learned what it was possible to learn about seven-, eight- and nine-year-old children by working with them; at the end of every single school year I know what I ought to have done. But when you have reached the fourth or fifth school year for the second time, again you will not know how you really ought to have taught. For now you will correct what you thought to be right after you had taught for a year. And so, after you have finished the eighth school year and have corrected everything, if you really have the good fortune to begin again in the first grade, you will find yourself in the same position—but now, to be sure, you will teach in a different spirit. If you carry out your teaching duties with inwardly true, noble, and not false doubts, you will find that your diffidence has brought you an imponderable power that will make you peculiarly fitted to accomplish more with the children entrusted to you. This is absolutely true. The effect in one's life, however, will really be only a different one—not one that is so much better, just different. I might say that the quality you bring about in the children will not be much better than the first time, the effect will only be different. You will attain something different in quality but not much more in quantity. You will attain something that is different in quality and that is sufficient, for everything we acquire in the way described, with the necessary noble diffidence and heartfelt humility, has the effect that we are able to make individualities out of human beings, individualities in the best sense of the word. We cannot have the same class twice and send out into the world the same copies of a cut-and-dried educational pattern. We can, however, give the world personalities who are individually different. We bring about diversity in life, but this does not derive from the working out of abstract principles. The diversity depends on the deeper understanding of life that we have just described.

You can see from all this that what matters more than anything else in a teacher is the way he or she regards this holy calling. This is not insignificant, for the most important things in teaching and in education are those that are imponderable. A teacher who enters the classroom with this heartfelt conviction achieves something different from one who does not. Just as in everyday life it is not always what is physically large that counts but something quite small, so it is not always what we do with big words that carries most weight. Sometimes it is the perception, the feeling that we have built up in our hearts before we enter the classroom.

One thing of special importance is that we must quickly strip off our narrow, personal self like a snakeskin when we enter the classroom. Teachers may go on through all sorts of experiences between the end of class one day and beginning again on the next because they are, as is sometimes said with such self-satisfaction, really only human. It may be that they have been pressed by their creditors, or have quarrelled with a spouse, as does happen. There are things that put us out of sorts. Such disharmonies provide an undertone to our state of soul, as do happy, joyous feelings as well. The father of a pupil who particularly likes you may have sent you a pheasant after he has been out hunting, or perhaps a bouquet of flowers. What I mean is that it is quite a natural thing to carry moods of this kind around with us. As teachers, however, we must train ourselves to lay aside these moods and give ourselves up entirely to the content of the subject we are going to teach. We should really be able to describe a subject tragically, taking our mood from the subject, and then pass over into a humorous mood as we proceed with our lesson, surrendering ourselves completely to the subject.

The important thing is that we should also be able to perceive the whole reaction of the class to tragedy or romance or humor. When we are able to do this, we shall become aware that all three moods are of extraordinary significance for the children's soul life. And if we allow our lessons to be carried along by an alternation of humor, romance, and tragedy, if we pass from one mood into the other and back again, if we are really able, after presenting something for which we needed a certain heaviness, to pass over into a certain lightness—not a forced lightness, but one that arises because we are living in our lesson—then we are bringing about in the children's soul life something akin to the in- and out-breathing of the bodily organism.

As we teach, our object is not simply to teach with and for the intellect, but rather to really be able to consider these various moods. For what is tragedy, what is romance, what is a "melancholic" mood? It is exactly the same as an in-breathing for the organism, the same as filling the organism with air. Tragedy means that we are trying harder and harder to draw our physical body together so that in doing so we become aware of the astral body emerging further and further out of it, owing to this contraction. A humorous mood signifies that we paralyze the physical body, but with the astral we do just the opposite of what we did before; we expand it as far as possible, spreading it out over its surroundings so that we are aware, for example, if we do not merely look at something red but move out into it, how we spread our astral body over this redness and pass over into it. Laughing simply means that we drive the astral body out of our facial features; it is nothing else but an astral out-breathing. If we want to apply all this in our teaching we must have a certain feeling for the dynamics. It is not always advisable on the heels of something heavy and sustained to go straight over into the humorous. However, we can always find the ways and means in our lessons to prevent the child's soul from being imprisoned by the serious or the tragic, and in extricating it, we will free it so that it can really breathe in and out between the two moods of soul.

These are some introductory examples of the variety of moods teachers should consider while teaching; certainly this is just as important as any other specific aspect of education.

2

The Three Fundamental Forces in Education

IT is naturally not possible to educate or give instruction without a kind of inward experiencing of the whole human being, for during children's development this whole human being needs to be considered far more carefully than later on. As we know, the whole human being comprises within itself the ego, the astral body, the etheric body, and the physical body. These four members of our nature by no means undergo a uniform development; they unfold in quite different ways. We must clearly distinguish between the development of the physical and the etheric bodies, and that of the astral body and the ego. The outer signs of this dissimilar development express themselves—as you know from various indications I have given here and there—in the change of teeth, and in the change that in the male appears as the change of voice at puberty, and also proclaims itself clearly in the female, though in a different way. The essence of the phenomenon is the same as the voice change in the male, only in the female organism it appears in a more diffused form, so that it is not observable in merely one organ, as in the case of the male, but extends over the entire organism. You know that between the change of teeth and the change of voice, or puberty, lies the period of teaching with which we are principally concerned in the elementary schools, but the careful teacher and educator must also pay close attention to the years following puberty.

Let us call to mind what the change of teeth signifies. Before the change of teeth—that is, between birth and the change of teeth—the physical and etheric bodies in the child's organism are strongly influenced by the nerve-sense system operating from above downward. Up to about the seventh year the physical body and the etheric body are most effectively influenced from the head. In the head are concentrated the forces that are particularly active in these years—that is, in the years when imitation plays such an important role. And what takes place in the formation of the remaining organism, trunk and limbs, is achieved through what rays down from the head to this other part, to the trunk and the limb organism, to the physical body and the etheric body. What radiates from the head into the physical and etheric bodies of the whole child right into the tips of the fingers and toes, this radiating from the head into the whole child is soul activity, even though it emanates from the physical body. It is the same soul activity that is later active in the soul as intelligence and memory. Only later on, after the change of teeth, children begin to think in such a way that their memories become more conscious. The whole change that takes place in the child's soul life shows that certain soul forces previously active in the organism become active as soul forces after the seventh year. The whole period up to the change of teeth, while the child is growing, makes use of the same forces that after the seventh year appear as intellectual forces.

Here you have an interplay between soul and body that is quite real; the soul emancipates itself in the seventh year and begins to function—no longer in the body, but independently. At this point, those forces that come newly into being in the body as soul forces begin to be active, and from the seventh year on they are at work well into the next incarnation. Then whatever radiates upward from the body is thrust back, whereas the forces that shoot downward from the head are restrained. Thus, during the time the teeth are changing, the most severe battle is fought between the forces striving downward from above and those shooting upward from below. The change of teeth is the physical expression of this conflict between the two kinds of forces: those that later appear in the child as powers of reasoning and intellect, and those that need to be used particularly in drawing, painting, and writing. We employ upwelling forces when we develop writing out of drawing, for what these forces really strive for is to pass over into sculptural formation, drawing, and so forth. These are the sculptural forces that, ending with the change of teeth, have previously modeled the child's body. We work with them later, when the second dentition is completed, to lead the child to drawing, to painting, and so on. These are primarily the forces that were placed into the child by the spiritual world in which the child's soul lived before conception. At first they are active as bodily forces in forming the head, and then from the seventh year on they function as soul forces. Therefore in the period following the seventh year, through authority in our teaching we simply draw forth what had earlier been unconsciously active in the child as imitation; at that time these forces had a strong unconscious influence on the body. If later the child becomes a sculptor, a draftsperson, or an architect—but a real architect who works out of formative principles—it is because such a person has the predisposition for retaining in his or her organism, specifically in the head, a little more of the forces that radiate downward into the organism, so that later on these forces of childhood can still radiate downward. But if they are entirely used up, if with the change of teeth everything passes over into the soul, then we will have children without a talent for drawing, sculpture, or architecture, who could never become sculptors.

This is the secret: these forces are related to what we have experienced between death and a new birth. The reverence that is needed to make education effective, something that can take on a religious quality, will arise if you as a teacher are conscious that when around the seventh year you call forth from the child's soul the forces that are used when the child learns to draw and to write, these actually come down from heaven! The child is the mediator, and you are actually working with forces sent down from the spiritual world. When this reverence for the divine-spiritual permeates your teaching, it truly works miracles. And if you have reverence, if you have the feeling that by means of this connection with forces developed in the spiritual world before birth—a feeling that engenders a deep reverence—you will see that through such a feeling you can accomplish more than through any amount of intellectual theorizing about what should be done. Reverence will have an immeasurable formative influence upon the child; the teacher's feelings are certainly the most important tools of education.

During the child's change of teeth, then, transference of spiritual forces is being enacted, forces that move from the spiritual world through the child and into the physical world.

Another process takes place in puberty, but it is prepared gradually through the whole cycle of years from the seventh to the fourteenth or fifteenth. During this time something is stirring to life in those regions of our soul that are not yet illuminated by consciousness. Something is radiating continuously into us from the outer world; we are unconscious of it, for our own consciousness is only now being formed. What since birth has permeated the child from the outer world, what has cooperated in building up the body and has entered into the child's formative forces is now gradually emerging into consciousness.

These are yet different forces; while the sculptural forces enter the head from within, these others now come from outside. Forcing their way through the sculptural forces and descending into the organism, they cooperate in what takes place, beginning with the seventh year, in building up the child's body. I can only characterize these forces as those active in speech and in music.

They are forces of a musical nature that we take up from the outer world, the world outside humankind, from our observation of nature and its processes, above all from observation of nature's regularities and irregularities. For everything going on in nature is permeated by a hidden music, the earthly projection of the "music of the spheres." Every plant, every animal actually incorporates a tone of the music of the spheres. This is also true of the human body: the music of the spheres still lives in the forms and structure of the body, but it no longer lives in human speech, expressing the soul nature.

All of this the child absorbs unconsciously, and for this reason children are so highly musical. They are taking all of this up into their bodily organism. What children experience as formed movement, as linear and sculptural elements, comes from within, from the head; what children absorb as tone texture, as speech content, comes from outside. Somewhat later, around the fourteenth year, what is coming from outside works against the gradually developing spiritual element of music and speech coming from within. A process of pressing them together—of compacting—takes place in the girl's whole organism, in the boy more in the region of the larynx, where it causes the change of voice. This process is brought about by an element from within, bearing more of the nature of will that runs up against a similar will element coming from outside; this conflict finds expression in the change of voice and the other changes at puberty. It is a battle between inner and outer forces of music and speech.

Up to the seventh year the human being is permeated on the whole more by sculptural and less by musical forces—that is, less by the inspiring music and speech forces that enkindle the whole organism. But beginning with the seventh year, music and speech become particularly active in the etheric body. Then the ego and the astral body turn against this; an element of will battles from outside against a similar will element from within, and this becomes apparent at puberty. The difference that exists between male and female has another outer manifestation in the difference of vocal pitch. The voice levels of a man and woman coincide only in part; the voice of the woman reaches higher, that of a man descends deeper into the bass. This corresponds precisely to the structure of the rest of the organism, formed out of the struggle between these forces.

All this shows that in our soul life we are concerned with something that at certain definite times also cooperates in the building up of the organism. All the abstract discussions you find in modern scientific books on psychology, all the talk about psychophysical parallelism, are testimony to the inability of our philosophers and psychologists to grasp the connection between the psychological and the physical. The psychological is certainly not connected with the physical in the manner set forth in the senseless theories thought out by the psychophysical parallelists. We should recognize the wholly concrete action of the psychological in the body and its reactions, one of which we will speak of shortly.

Up to the seventh year the sculptural element works together with the music and speech elements; then there is a change, so that from the seventh year the relation between music and speech on the one hand and the sculptural on the other is a different one. But through the whole period up to puberty this cooperation takes place between the sculptural, which emanates from the head and has its seat there, and music and speech, which come from outside, using the head as a conduit, and spread themselves into the organism.

From this we see that human language, particularly its musical element, cooperates in shaping the human being. First it forms us, then it stems itself, pausing at the larynx so that it does not pass this entrance gate as it did before. For before, you see, it has been speech that changed our organs, even down into the bony system. And anyone who observes a human skeleton from a genuine psychophysical point of view—not with the absurd psychophysical thoughts of our contemporary philosophers and psychologists—and considers the differences between the male and the female skeleton, will see in the skeleton an embodied piece of music performed by the reciprocal action of the human organism and the outer world. Were we to play a sonata and preserve its structure through some spiritual process of crystallization, we would have, as it were, the principal forms, the scheme of arrangement, of the human skeleton! And that will, incidentally, attest to the difference between human beings and animals. Whatever the animal absorbs of the music and speech element—very little of the speech, but very much of the musical—passes through the animal, because in a sense the animal lacks the human isolation that later leads to mutation. In the shape of an animal skeleton we also have a musical imprint, but a composite of different animal skeletons, such as one finds, for instance, in a museum, is needed to provide a complete musical impression. An animal invariably manifests a onesidedness in its structure.

We ought to consider such things carefully; they will show us what feelings we should develop in forming our picture of the human being. Just as our reverence grows if we cultivate our connection and attunement with prenatal forces, we will acquire greater enthusiasm for teaching by immersing ourselves in other human forces. A Dionysian element irradiates, as it were, the music and speech instruction, while we have more of an Apollonian element in teaching sculpture, painting, and drawing. The instruction that has to do with music and speech we will impart with enthusiasm; the other we will give with reverence.

The sculptural forces offer the stronger opposition; hence they are arrested as early as the seventh year. The other forces, counteracting less vigorously, are arrested only in the fourteenth year. You must not take this to mean physical strength and weakness;

I am referring to the counter pressure that is exerted. Since the sculptural forces, being stronger, would overwhelm the human organism, the counter pressure is greater. Therefore they must be arrested earlier, whereas the musical forces are permitted by cosmic guidance to remain longer in the organism. The human being is permeated longer by the musical forces than by the sculptural.

If you let this thought ripen within you and bring the requisite enthusiasm to bear, conscious that by developing an appreciation for speech and music precisely during the elementary school period, when the struggle we referred to is still raging and when you are still influencing the bodily nature—not just the soul nature—then you are preparing what will have an effect and be carried even beyond death. We are contributing essentially to this through everything we impart to the child in the way of music and speech during the elementary school period. And this should give us a certain enthusiasm, because we know that thereby we are working for the future. On the other hand, by working with sculptural forces we are in touch with what already lay in the human being before birth, before conception, and this gives us reverence.

We combine our own forces with those that reach into the future and realize that we are fructifying the germ of music and speech with something that will have its effect on these in the future after the physical has been cast off. Music itself reflects the music of the spheres in the air—only thus does it become physical. The air is in a sense the medium in which tones become physical, just as it is the air in the larynx that makes speech physical. It is the non-physical in the air used in speech and the non-physical in the air used in music that unfold their true activity only after death. That is what brings about our enthusiasm for teaching, for we know that we are working into the future.

I believe that in the future people will no longer talk to teachers about education as they usually do today, but rather in ideas and concepts that can be transformed into feelings. For nothing is more important than that we are able as teachers to develop the necessary reverence, the necessary enthusiasm, so that we can teach with reverence and enthusiasm. Reverence and enthusiasm—these are the two secret and fundamental forces that must permeate the teacher's soul with spirit.

To help you understand all this better, I should like to mention that the musical element is at home principally in the astral body. After death we still carry our astral body with us for a time; and as long as that is so, until we lay it aside completely—you are familiar with this from my book, *Theosophy*—there still exists in us after death a kind of recollection (it is no more than a memory) of earthly music. In this way the music we receive during our life works on as a musical memory after death—until about the time the astral body is laid aside. Then in the life after death the earthly music is transformed into the music of the spheres, and it remains as such until some time before a new birth.

This will be more comprehensible to you if you know that the music we take in here on Earth plays a powerful role in shaping our soul organism after death, during the period of kamaloka.[3] This is the comforting feature of the kamaloka time, and if we know this, we are essentially in a position to ease for people what the Roman Catholics call the fires of purgatory. Not, to be sure, by removing their contemplation of it, which they must have. They would remain imperfect if they could not observe the imperfect things they have done. But we introduce the possibility that human beings will be better formed in their next life if during the time after death, when they still have their astral body, they can have many memories of musical experiences. This can be studied

---

3. The period after death when the soul is freeing itself from its inclination toward physical existence in order to follow the laws of the spiritual world. See *Theosophy*, chapter 3 or *An Outline of Esoteric Science*, chapter 3.

at a comparatively low stage of spiritual knowledge. You need only wake up in the night after having heard a concert and you will be aware that you have experienced the whole concert again before waking. You even experience it much better when waking in the night after the concert; the experience is very accurate. The point is that music imprints itself upon the astral body, it remains there, it still resonates; it remains for about thirty years after death. Music continues to resonate much longer than speech; we lose the latter comparatively quickly after death, and only its spiritual extract remains. What is musical is preserved as long as the astral body. The essence of speech can be a great gift to us after death, especially if we have often absorbed it in the form I now frequently describe as the art of recitation. When I describe the latter in this way, I naturally have every reason to point out that these things cannot be rightly understood without keeping in view the peculiar course the astral body takes after death; matters must then be described somewhat as I have done in my lectures on eurythmy.[4] Here, you see, we must talk to people in more or less primitive language, and it is really true that, seen from the point of view beyond the threshold, everyone is actually primitive; only beyond the threshold are they real human beings. And we can only work ourselves out of this primitive state by working our way into spiritual reality. This is also the reason for the constantly increasing and primitive fury against the endeavors of anthroposophy.

Now I would like to point out something that should have our particular attention in the art of education, something that can be useful there—namely, that a certain characteristic is to be noted in what I described as the first conflict in the child, whose outer expression is the change of teeth, and in the later struggle

---

4. Rudolf Steiner, *An Introduction to Eurythmy*, Anthroposophic Press, NY, 1984.

whose equivalent is the change of voice. Everything that descends from the head until the seventh year appears as an attack on what is coming to the child from within in the nature of upbuilding forces. And everything that works outward from within upward to the head, countering the stream emanating from the head, is like a defense opposed to the downward stream, which could be considered as an attack.

It is similar in the case of music, but here what comes from within appears as an attack, and what descends from above through the head organism appears as the defense. If we did not have music, frightful forces would actually rise up in us. I am completely convinced that up to the sixteenth or seventeenth century, traditions deriving from the ancient mysteries were active, and that even then people still wrote and spoke under the influence of this aftereffect of the mysteries. They no longer knew, to be sure, the whole meaning of this effect, but in much that still appears in comparatively recent times, we simply have remnants of the old mystery wisdom.

Hence I have always been deeply impressed by the words of Shakespeare: "The man that hath no music in himself... is fit for treasons, stratagems, and spoils!... Let no such man be trusted."[5]

In the old mystery schools the pupils were told that what acts as an attack from within us and must be continually warded off, what is dammed back for the sake of human nature, is "treasons, stratagems, and spoils," and that the music that is active in us is what counteracts it. Music is our defense against the luciferic forces rising up out of the inner human being: disloyalty, murder, and deceit. We all have disloyalty, murder, and deceit within us, and it is not without reason that the world contains what comes to us from music and speech, quite aside from the pleasure it affords.

---

5. *The Merchant of Venice*, Act 5, Scene 1.

Its purpose is to make people into human beings. One must, of course, keep in mind that the old mystery teachers expressed themselves somewhat differently; they expressed things more concretely. They would not have said "treasons, stratagems, and spoils" (it is already toned down in Shakespeare), but would have said something like "serpent, wolf, and fox." The serpent, the wolf, and the fox are warded off from the inner nature of the human being through music. The old mystery teachers would always have used animal forms to depict what rises up within us but must then be transformed into what is human. So it is that we can achieve the right enthusiasm when we see the treacherous serpent rising out of the child and combat it with music and speech instruction, and in the same way contend with the murderous wolf and the tricky fox or cat. That is what can then permeate us with true, intelligent enthusiasm—not the burning, luciferic sort that alone is acknowledged today.

In recognizing the interplay between attack and defense, we must remember that defense occurs in us on two levels. The first is within ourselves, where a warding off appears in the change of teeth in the seventh year. The second is what we have received from music and speech when this wards off what tends to rise up within us. Both battlefields are within the human being; what comes from music and speech is more toward the periphery, toward the outer world, and the sculptural tends more toward the inner world.

But there is still a third battlefield, and that lies on the boundary between the etheric body and the outer world. The etheric body is always larger than the physical body, reaching out beyond it in all directions, and here too is a battlefield. Here the battle is fought more consciously, whereas the other two proceed more in the subconscious. This third and more conscious battle reveals itself when the other battles—the exchange between the human being and the sculptural on the one hand and what pertains to speech and music on the other hand—work themselves out and become a part of the etheric body. Taking hold of the astral body, this new force then moves more toward the periphery or outer boundary.

From this originates everything that shoots through our fingers when we draw, paint, and so on. Painting is an art, therefore, that works more in our environment. The draftsperson, the sculptor, must work more out of inner faculties, the musician more out of devotion to the world. What presents itself in painting and drawing, to which we lead the children when we have them draw forms and lines, is the battle that takes place wholly on the surface; it is fought principally between two forces, one working inward from outside, the other working outward from within. The force working outward from within actually tends to constantly spread a person out, tends to continue the formation of the human being—not violently, but in a delicate way. This force—I must express it more drastically than it really is, but in this exaggeration you will see what I mean—this force, working outward from within, tends to make our eyes bulge out, wants to give us a goiter, to make our nose puff out and to make the ears bigger; everything tends to swell outward.

Another force is present, however—one we absorb from the outer world that wards off this swelling. And even if we only draw a line—draw something—this is an effort to divert, through this force working in from the outer world, that inner force which is trying to deform us. It is a complicated reflex action, then, that we execute in painting, in drawing, in graphic activity. In drawing or in having the canvas before us, a feeling is actually glimmering in our consciousness that we are rebuffing something that is out there, that in the forms and lines we are setting up thick walls or barbed wire. In drawing we really have such barbed wire by means of which we quickly catch something swelling that tends to destroy us from within, preventing its action from becoming too strong. Therefore drawing instruction works best if it is based on a study of the human being. If you study the motions the hand tends to make—if, say, in eurythmy classes you have the children hold the motions, the gestures they want to carry out—then you have arrested the motion, the line that tends to destroy, and it does not act destructively. So when you begin to have the children draw eurythmic forms and then see that drawing and also writing are formed out of the will that lives in gesture, you have something that human nature really wants, something linked with its being and becoming.

In connection with eurythmy we should know that in our etheric body we constantly have the tendency to do eurythmy; it is something the etheric body simply does of its own accord, for eurythmy is nothing but motions gleaned from what the etheric body tends to do of itself. It is really the etheric body that makes these motions, and it is only prevented from doing so when we cause the physical body to carry them out. When we allow them to be made by the physical body, these movements are checked in the etheric body but react upon us, this time with a health-giving effect.

These are things that affect the human being both in a curative-therapeutic and an educational way. They will be understood only when we know that whatever is trying to manifest itself in the etheric organization must be stopped at the periphery by the movements of the physical body. In the case of eurythmy an element more connected with the will is stopped; in drawing and painting, it is an element more closely allied with the intellect. Fundamentally, both are two poles of the same thing.

If we feel our way into this process and incorporate it into our sensitive capacity as teachers, we will arrive at the third feeling we need, which should permeate us through all our work in the elementary school: when children come into the world, they are exposed to things that we must protect them from through our teaching. Otherwise they would flow too actively into the world.

A person always has the tendency to become weak and stunted in soul, to make rachitic limbs, to become a gnome. And in teaching and educating someone, we work at forming an individual. We sense this formative activity best if we observe the child making a drawing and we smooth it out a bit so that the result is not only what the child wants, and not exactly what we want either, but the result of both. If I can do this—improve what the child scribbles with his or her fingers—in merging my feelings with the child, the best results will come of it. And if I transform all this into a feeling and let it permeate me, it will be the feeling that I must protect the child from being absorbed too strongly by the outer world. We must see that the children grow slowly into the outer world and not let them do it too rapidly. We constantly hold a protecting hand over the child; this is the third feeling we teachers must cherish.

Reverence, enthusiasm, and a sense of guardianship, these three are actually the panacea, the magic remedy, in the soul of the educator and teacher. And if one wished to represent externally, artistically, something like an embodiment of art and education in a harmonious group, one would have to create it like this:

Reverence for what precedes the child's existence before birth;
Enthusiastic anticipation of what follows it, after death;
Protective gesture for what the child experiences during life.[6]

In this formulation the outward manifestation of the teacher's nature also comes to expression.

---

6. Rudolf Steiner accompanied each of these phrases with a gesture. The following description is attributed to Caroline von Heydebrandt: the gesture for reverence, hands folded in prayer (in the stenographic record: two hands inclining upward with the finger tips toward each other); the gesture for enthusiasm, hand outstretched, pointing; the protective feeling, the right arm [encircling] as in the eurythmy gesture for "B."

In speaking of such matters, drawn from the intimacies of world mysteries, we sense how unsatisfactory it must always be to use conventional language. If one must say such things in ordinary language, one always has the feeling that a corollary or supplement is needed. What is spoken more abstractly always wants to pass over into the artistic. That is why I wanted to make this final point.

We must learn to carry within us something that everyone in the future will feel: the possession of science alone makes the human being into what resembles a dwarf in soul and spirit. A scientist pure and simple will not have the impulse—not even in the forming of his or her thoughts—to transform the scientific into the artistic. But only through the artistic do we grasp the world. Goethe's words will always be true: "He to whom Nature begins to reveal her manifest secrets feels an irresistible longing for her most worthy interpreter, Art."

As educators we should be able to perceive that as far as you are only a scientist, you might as well be an ignoramus! Not until you have transformed your organism of soul, spirit, and body, when your knowledge assumes an artistic form, will you become a human being. Our future development—and in this teachers will have to play their part—will lead from science to artistic understanding, from a deformed being to the attainment of full humanity.

3

Supersensible Physiology in Education

STUTTGART — SEPTEMBER 21, 1920

IT is essential in life to have the relationships with our surroundings in proper order. We can eat and digest suitable foods furnished by the outside world, but we would be poorly nourished if we ate food already partially digested by other people. The important point is that when we receive things from outside us in a definite form, they acquire value for our life because we need to work on them. It is the same at higher levels too, for example, in the art of education. Here the important thing is to know first what we should learn and then, in the light of what we have learned, what we ourselves must actually invent in handling our class. If one studies education as a science consisting of all sorts of principles and formulas, it means about the same thing in terms of education as choosing to eat partially digested foods. But if we undertake a study of the child, of the true nature of the human being, and learn to understand children in this way, we take into ourselves the equivalent of what nature offers us as nourishment. And in the practice of teaching there will awaken in us, out of this knowledge of human nature, the art of education in a quite individual form. In reality the teacher must invent this art every moment. That is the point I wished to make as an introduction to today's talk.

In teaching and education there is a curious interweaving of two different elements: the musical, tonal element that we hear in the world, and the pictorial in the world that we see. Of course, other sense impressions are intermingled with what we hear and what we see, and these can at times have a secondary importance for the lesson, but they do not have the same significance as seeing and hearing.

It is essential that we really understand what is actually going on right down into the body. You know that modern science distinguishes two kinds of nerves in the human being, the so-called sensory nerves, which are supposed to run from the sense organs to the brain or central nervous system, from which they transmit perceptions and mental images, and the motor nerves, which are supposed to run from the central nervous system to the organs of movement, setting these in motion. You know that from the point of view of spiritual science we have to challenge this classification. There is absolutely no difference between the so-called sensory nerves and motor nerves. Both are one and the same—the motor nerves primarily serve no other purpose than to make us aware of the moving limbs and the actual process of motion the moment it happens. They have nothing to do with stimulating the will. Therefore we can say that we have nerves running from our periphery more toward the center and we have nerves running from the center to the ends of the organs of motion, but fundamentally these are one and the same nerve strands. The essential point is only that there is an interruption between these equivalent nerves, so that the active soul current, streaming through a "sensory" nerve to the center, for instance, is interrupted, as it were, at the center and there must jump across. (This is very much like the passage of an electric spark or current that jumps across an electric switch when the transmission is inter-rupted.) It is a jump to the so-called motor nerve, which does not change at this moment but remains the same as a sensory nerve, except in one respect: the motor nerve is capable of becoming aware of motion and of the moving limbs.

There is something that can give us an intimate insight into this whole organic process in which soul currents and bodily happenings interact. Let us assume, as a starting point, that we are looking at a picture, that is, a perception conveyed primarily through the sense organ of sight—a drawing, a form or shape of something in our surroundings—in short, anything that becomes a possession of our soul through our eyes. We must now distinguish three distinctly different inner activities that occur at this moment.

First we have *perception* as such; this perception takes place within the organ of sight. Secondly, we must distinguish *comprehension*, and here we should be clear that all comprehension is transmitted through our rhythmic system, not through the nerve-sense system, which transmits only perception. We comprehend what a picture is, for instance, only through the fact that the rhythmic activity, regulated by the heart and lungs, is carried through the cerebrospinal fluid up to the brain. In reality, comprehension is transmitted physically by the rhythms that occur in the brain and have their origin in our rhythmic system. It is through breathing that we are able to comprehend.

How mistakenly these things are generally considered by physiology today! It is believed that comprehension has something to do with the human nervous system, whereas in actuality it is based on the fact that the rhythmic system receives what we perceive and forms a mental picture of it, and then works further on it. Because the rhythmic system is linked with our comprehension, the latter is closely related to our feeling. Those of us who study and observe ourselves carefully will see the connection between comprehension and emotion. Actually, we have to feel the truth of something we have understood if we are to agree with it. It is our rhythmic system that supplies the meeting place for our comprehending knowledge and the soul's element of feeling.

There is still a third aspect: to take in what comes to us in such a way that our memory can retain it. With every event we have to identify perception, comprehension, and an inward working over of what we have understood so that our memory retains it. This third element is linked with the metabolic system; the most delicate inner metabolic processes going on in the organism are connected with memory, with the capacity for remembering.

We must pay very careful attention to these processes, for as teachers we have particular reason to know about them. Notice what a different kind of memory pale children have compared with children who have nice rosy cheeks, or how different with regard to memory the various human races are. Everything of this kind is dependent on the delicate organization and processes of the metabolism. We can, for example, strengthen the memory of pale children if, as teachers, we are in a position to see that they sleep soundly, so that the delicate processes of their metabolism receive greater stimulation. Another way of helping their memory would be to bring about for them in our teaching a balanced rhythm between mere listening and working on their own. Suppose you let the children listen too much. They will manage to pay attention and they will also understand, if they're pushed, for they're breathing all the time and therefore keeping their brain fluid moving—but their will is not being sufficiently exerted. The will, as you know, is connected with the metabolism. If you let the children get too much into the habit of watching and listening without doing enough work by themselves, you will not be able to teach them properly; mental assimilation is connected with the metabolism and will—and the will is not active enough. You will have to find the right balance between the children's listening and watching on the one hand, and having to exert themselves independently on the other. The result of the children's working over by themselves what they have seen and heard is that their will works into the metabolism and enkindles memory. These are subtle physiological matters that will have to be grasped very exactly by means of spiritual science.

All this has referred to the pictorial element, the visual experience of sight; it is quite different in the case of everything that relates to the element of sound, to the more or less musical element. I do not only mean the musical element that lives in music, which serves as the clearest and best example, but everything to do with what we hear, with what lives musically in language, and so forth. I include all of that when I speak now of sound. However paradoxical it may seem, the process here is the exact reverse of the one just described. The sense organization in the ear is inwardly linked in a very delicate way with all those nerves known to modern physiology as motor nerves, which are in fact identical to the sensory nerves; everything we experience as resonating sound is perceived through the nerve strands embedded in our limb organism. Everything musical, if it is to be perceived properly, must first penetrate deeply into our whole organism—and for this the nerves of the ear are suitably arranged—and then it must seize hold where the nerves are otherwise reached only by the will. Those regions in the human organism that convey memory of pictorial experiences are the very ones that in the case of the musical, audible element give rise to perception. Therefore if you look for the area in the organism where memory of visible perceptions is developed, you will also find the nerves that convey the actual perception of sound. That is the reason, for instance, why Schopenhauer connected music so intimately with the will. The will zones, where visual images are remembered, are also the place where the perception of sound as mental image arises.

The comprehension of sound as mental image also takes place in the rhythmic system. That is what is so impressive about the human organism, that these things intertwine in such a remarkable way. Our visual images meet with our audible images and weave themselves into a common inner soul experience because they are both comprehended by means of the rhythmic system.

Everything we perceive is comprehended by means of the rhythmic system; visual images are perceived by the isolated head organism; audible images are perceived by the whole limb organism. Visual images stream inward toward the organism; audible images stream from the organism upward.

You must combine all this with what I said in the first lecture. If you are sensitive enough, it is not difficult to make the connection. Through the fact that the two worlds meet in the rhythmic system, something arises in our soul that comprises both sound experiences and sight experiences. The musical—everything audible—is remembered in the same region where the visible has its sensory nerve organs. These are at one and the same time the organs that appear to be sensory nerve organs, as ordinary physiology calls them, but in reality they are connected with the metabolism; they convey the delicate metabolism of the head region and bring about musical memories. In the same region where the perception of visible images arises, musical memory—in fact, the memory of anything audible—comes about as well. In the same regions where we perceive the visible, we remember the audible. In the same regions where we remember the visible, we perceive the audible. And the two cross over each other like a lemniscate in the rhythmic system, where they dovetail and interlock.

Anyone who has ever studied musical memory—a wonderful and mysterious thing, even though we all take it for granted— will find out how fundamentally different it is from the memory of something visible. This memory for music is based on a particular, delicate organization of the head metabolism; in its general character it is also related to the will, and therefore to the metabolism. Music memory and the memory of visual images are located in different regions of the body; both, however, are connected with the will.

When you have reflected on these things, you will be impressed by how complicated the speech process is. Because the rhythmic system is so closely linked with the speech organism, comprehension comes about when the speech process unfolds from within and works outward. It comes to expression in a remarkable way, and in order to make it clear I should like to remind you of Goethe's theory of color. Besides calling the red-yellow half of the color world "warm" and the blue-violet part "cold," Goethe brings color perception and tone perception closely together. He sees, as it were, a different kind of "sounding" in the red-yellow portion of the spectrum from that in the blue-violet part, and this connects, for instance, with major and minor in music— that is, with certain more intimate aspects of tone experience. You can find this in those of his writings on natural science that were published from the unprinted material of the Weimar edition, and were then added to the last volume of my Kürschner edition.[7] We can certainly say that if we look into ourselves at these inner processes in the same way that Goethe looks at and describes the theory of color, we arrive at something remarkable. It is within the human being, it is in speech that sound comes to life. Indeed, the element of sound lives in speech but the sound is modified in a definite way. I might say it is permeated by something that "dulls it down" when we speak. This is not just a metaphor; we have to do with actual processes when we say that in speech the real *tone* has "color." The same thing happens within us as it does in the case of external color when we perceive it "tonally"—we do not actually perceive tone in external color, but in a sense we hear something sounding out of every color; the same occurs inwardly when we listen. We do not see a color when we pronounce "ee" or "oo," any more than we hear tones when we see yellow or blue; but we have the same experience when we feel color as we have in sound when we hear the tones of speech. Here the world of

---

7. Cf. especially vol. 4, part 2, pp.102 etc., of Goethe's *Naturwissenschaftliche Schriften*, edited by Rudolf Steiner (Goethe to Johann Leonhard Hoffman).

sight and the world of sound interpenetrate each other. The color we see outside in the world has obvious visual qualities, but also a subtle tone quality that enters us in the way I described in a previous talk. Speech coming from within us toward the surface has an obvious tone quality, but also has a subtle color quality in the various sounds, which rises upward to expression particularly in children up to the seventh year, as I have told you. From this you see that color is more pronounced in the outer world and sound is more pronounced in the human inner world; cosmic music moves beneath the surface in the outer world while beneath the surface of sound within the human being there streams and moves a mysterious astral element of color.

And now, if you rightly comprehend the marvelous living organism that comes forth from the human being as actual speech, you will feel, when you hear it, all the rhythms of the astral body within the colorful air movements that pass directly over into the words that sound forth from us. These rhythms are, of course, also active in us in other ways, but here they become strangely agitated, concentrate themselves toward the larynx and receive their impulses, for instance, from sun and moon. All this produces a certain play of forces in the astral body that comes to external expression in the movements of the larynx. Now you have the possibility to at least picture this: as you listen to any kind of language, observe, if you can, the astral body, which at once passes its rhythms on to the etheric body, making the whole process more inward. If you could draw a picture of all this, you would get only the intrinsic movements found in the human organism; that is the eurythmy that is always being carried out together by our astral and etheric bodies when we speak. There is nothing arbitrary here; you would merely be making visible what otherwise is constantly taking place invisibly.

Why would we do this at the present time? Because today we must do consciously what we formerly did unconsciously; the development of the human being consists in gradually bringing down into the sense world what originally only existed in the supersensible. The Greeks, for example, really still thought with their soul; their thinking was entirely of a soul nature. Modern human beings, especially since the middle of the fifteenth century, think with their brain. Materialism is a perfectly correct theory when applied to modern human beings, for what the Greeks still experienced in the soul has gradually imprinted itself on the brain and has become hereditary in the brain from generation to generation. Today human beings have started to think by means of the brain's imprints. They already think by material processes—in short, they think materialistically. That had to come. However, we must work our way upward again; we must add to these material processes by lifting ourselves to what comes from the supersensible world. We now have to do the opposite of what occurred when the soul was formerly imprinted into the body; that is, we have to take hold—in freedom—of the spiritual-supersensible through spiritual science. If the development of humanity is to progress, we must undertake this consciously, this bringing down of the supersensible into the sense world. We must consciously bring the human body, this body of the senses, into visible movement in a way that up to the present occurred invisibly, unconsciously. We shall be consciously continuing along the path of the gods if we take over their work of imprinting thought upon the brain and convert supersensible eurythmy into sense-perceptible eurythmy. Should we fail to do this, humankind would gradually sink into daydreams, would become somnolent. Things would come to such a pass that although various influences would flow from the spiritual worlds into the human ego and astral body, this would happen only during sleep, and on awakening these influences would never be transmitted to the physical body.

When people do eurythmy, through their movements the physical organism becomes a receptive organ for the spiritual world, for the movements that want to come down from there. By preparing themselves for this, eurythmists become receptive to what is directed out of the spiritual world. For the audience, the movements living in their astral body and ego are intensified through experiencing eurythmy movements in visible form. If you were suddenly to wake up in the night after a eurythmy performance, you would find that you felt much more satisfaction inwardly than if you had awakened after hearing a sonata at an evening concert. Eurythmy has an even stronger effect; it strengthens the soul by bringing it into living contact with the supersensible. A certain healthy balance, however, must be maintained, for if you have too much of it, the soul will fidget about in the spiritual world at night when one should sleep, and this restlessness in the soul would be the counterpart of physical nervousness.

You see how such things suggest an ever more real and active perception of this marvelous structure, our human organism. We become aware, on the one hand, that nothing exists in our body that is not permeated with spirit; on the other hand we see that the spirit and the soul aspire not to remain separated from physical experience. And it is especially interesting to allow everything I have presented today to work on you; let it invigorate you. For instance, in active meditation you can form for yourself a mental image of the musical life within us in the will region of visual experience; then meditate further on the existence of musical memory in the thought region of visual experience—and vice versa, connect what is in the region where we have mental images of the audible with what is in the region of the memory of visual experience. If you bring all these things together and form mental images of them in active meditation, you can be sure that the vigorous power of ingenuity you need when facing the children you are educating will be kindled in you.

Ideas like these, stemming from a spiritual-scientific method of education, have as their aim a more intimate knowledge of the human being. When you meditate on them, you cannot halt their continued effect within yourself. You see, when you eat a piece of bread and butter, first you are aware of a conscious action; but what takes place when the bread and butter pass through the complicated process of digestion is something you can affect very little, yet this process takes its course and your general well-being is closely bound up with it. Now if you study physiology as we have done you experience it consciously to start with, but if you meditate upon it afterward, an inner process of digestion goes on in your soul and spirit, and that is what makes you an educator and teacher. A healthy metabolic process makes an active human being out of you, and in the same way this meditative digestion of a true knowledge of the human being makes you an educator. You simply face the children as their teacher in an entirely different way if you have experienced what results from a genuine, spiritual-scientific knowledge of the human being. What makes us into educators actually grows out of the meditative work of acquiring such knowledge. Such observations as we have made today, if we keep returning to them if only for five minutes a day, will bring our inner soul life into movement. We shall produce so many thoughts and feelings that they will just pour out of us. Meditate in the evening upon such knowledge of the human being and in the morning you will know in a flash, "Of course, this or that is what I must do with Johnnie Miller," or, "This girl needs this or that," and so on. In short, you will know what to do in every case.

In our human life it is important to bring about this sort of cooperation between inner and outer experiences. You do not even need much time for it. Once you have got the knack, in three seconds you can get an inner grasp of things that will keep you going for a whole day's teaching. Time loses its significance when it is a matter of bringing the supersensible to life. The spirit simply has different laws. Just as everything contracts in a dream, things we receive from the spirit can expand. In the same way, on waking up you can have a thought whose time-content could fill weeks but shoots through your mind in no time at all: so permeating yourself through meditation with this spiritual-scientific knowledge of the human being can bring you to the point when you have reached your fortieth or forty-fifth year to carrying out in five minutes the whole inner transformation that you need for your teaching. You will be quite different then in ordinary life from what you were before.

One can read about such things in the writings of those who have experienced them. You can begin to understand them, but you must also understand that what is experienced by a few individuals to an especially high degree, in a way that can then throw light upon the whole of life, must take place on a smaller scale in the teacher's case.

As teachers we must take up for ourselves the study of the human being; we must come to a comprehension of the human being through meditation; we must keep in our memory the nature of the human being—then the memory will become vigorous life. It is not the usual kind of remembering, but one that gives new inner impulses. In this instance memory wells forth from the life of the spirit and carries initiatives over into our external work. This is the third stage. Meditative comprehension is followed by active, creative remembering, which is at the same time a receiving of what emanates from the spiritual world. We start with an acceptance or perception of knowledge of the human being; then comes comprehension, a meditative comprehension of this knowledge that becomes inward and is received by the whole of our rhythmic system; finally, we have a remembering of the knowledge of the human being out of the spirit. This means teaching creatively out of the spirit; the art of education comes about and takes form. This must become a conviction, must become a direction of soul.

You have to see the human being in such a way that you constantly feel these three stages within yourself. The more you are able to say to yourself: there is my physical body, there is my skin; they enclose the being who receives the knowledge of the human being, who meditatively comprehends it, whom God has blessed and invigorated through remembering it—the more you have this feeling within you, the more you will be a genuine teacher.

4

Balance in Teaching

STUTTGART — SEPTEMBER 22, 1920

WHEN we look at human beings and observe how they are constituted, and then apply this knowledge to the child, the developing human being, the following picture comes to us. Out of the spiritual world into this one comes—we could say, on astral wings— the human ego being. Observing children in the early years of life, how they develop; how by degrees they bring their physiognomy from the depth of their inner being to the body's surface; how they gain more and more control over their organism; what we see in this process is essentially the incorporation of the ego. What really takes place here can be characterized in different ways, two of which are already familiar to you.

I have recently emphasized how the organizing principle in the physical body emerges with the change of teeth, frees itself during this time, and shapes primarily the intelligence. That is one way of describing the process. Another way, however, stated earlier when the whole subject was brought to our understanding from a different standpoint, is to say that the etheric body is born with the change of teeth. The first birth is of the physical body but the birth of the etheric body is not until about the seventh year. What we call the birth of the etheric or formative force body can also be seen as the emancipation of the intelligence from the physical body, a two-sided description of the same phenomenon. We can grasp the matter only by observing two such aspects at the same time. In spiritual science nothing can be characterized without approaching something from different sides and then combining the different aspects into one comprehensive view. Just as little as a single tone comprises a melody can a single characterization be enough for what spiritual science describes. You must characterize from different angles. In former times people who understood something about this called it "hearing the various explanations sound together."

What else happens? Into the etheric body or intelligence, whichever you like to call it, into what has become free streams the ego, which had already descended at birth and now works on the etheric body, bringing it gradually into shape. In this period, therefore, an intermingling takes place between the eternal ego and the slowly liberated intelligence or nascent etheric body.

If we consider the next period, from the seventh year to the fourteenth, or puberty, we can say that in a sense an element of will, a musical element, is being absorbed. Described from this angle, what happens is best described by the word "absorbed," for the musical element really has its being in the outer world. The musical tone element being absorbed is indeed permeated by a pulsating, vibrating impulse coming from what spiritual science calls the astral forces. Thereby the astral organism becomes freed from its former connection with the child's total organization. We can then say with regard to the child that at puberty the birth of the astral body takes place. But again it is the ego, the eternal element, that unites itself with what is being freed, so that from birth to puberty—that is, up to the age of fourteen or later—we have a continuous anchoring of the ego in the entire human organization. After the seventh year the ego settles itself only into the etheric body, whereas previously, while the human being was still an imitator—indeed, due precisely to this imitative activity—it worked itself into the physical body, and later, after puberty, it establishes itself in the astral body. What we have then is a continuous penetration of the human organization by the ego.

This whole array of facts has an immense significance for the educator. Fundamentally speaking, all teaching and instruction should constantly keep in view this integration of the ego into the rest of the human organization as I have just described it. The process of ego integration should be guided by an artistic education, as I have indicated in an essay on education in the journal *The Threefold Social Order*.[8]

What do I mean by this? I mean, for example, that the ego must not be permitted to enter the physical, the etheric, or the astral body too deeply, nor must it be too much excluded. When the former occurs, when it combines too intensely with the human organism, people become too materialistic. We will then think only with our brain, will be wholly dependent upon our organism; we become too much body. The ego is unduly absorbed by the organism, and this we must prevent through education. We must try to avoid everything that permits the ego to be too strongly absorbed by the organism or to become too dependent on it. You will understand how serious this is when I tell you that the cause of the criminality and brutality in people lies in the fact that their ego was allowed to be too strongly absorbed while they were growing up. When this has occurred, anthropologists confirm what are called symptoms of degeneracy in criminals, but these symptoms are frequently not discovered until they are well developed in later life, revealing that the ego of these people had become too deeply embedded in the rest of the organism. In the case of a child born with so-called "criminal earlobes," it is all the more necessary to take special care that this does not

8. See "The Pedagogical Basis of the Waldorf School" in *The Renewal of the Social Organism* (*Aufsätze über die Dreigliederung des sozialen Organismus und zur Zeitlage*, GA 24), Anthroposophic Press, Spring Valley, NY, 1985.

happen. By means of truly artistic educational methods we can prevent the ego from settling too deeply in the child's organism if there are symptoms of degeneracy. We can save such children from becoming criminals.

We can, on the other hand, make the opposite mistake. The difficulty here is like using the balances in scales: we can place too much or too little weight on one side, and then we have to set the balance right. It is just like this with facts confronting us in life. In trying to rectify a mistake we may easily fall into the opposite error. Living reality can never be expressed in rigid concepts, and in dealing with a child it is the intimate elements of life that are all-important. We must never develop one extreme or the other in a one-sided way but rather the feeling that in education one has to create an artistic balance.

When the teacher fails to induce a rightful fusion of the ego with the rest of the organization, it can then happen that the ego remains too far outside, with the result that the child becomes a dreamer or a visionary, or someone who will be generally useless in the world, living in the grip of fantasies. That is the other extreme, the mistake of not letting the ego sink deeply enough into the organism. But even children with a predisposition for dreaming, for false romanticism, for theosophy in the wrong sense, can be saved from becoming fanatics unable to cope with life if the educator sees to it that the ego is not unduly excluded from the rest of the organism but permeates it in the right way. When one finds in a child the well-known characteristic of theosophists, a small bump rising a little way behind the forehead that all children inclined to theosophy bring with them, the important thing is to discourage the tendency to faddism and sentimentality by pressing the ego more strongly into the organism.

But how can we achieve these two necessary results? We can accomplish something in both directions by discovering the methods to cope with such needs, and these are the following:

Everything in teaching that requires one to form mental images of number and space, like geometry and arithmetic, helps the ego to settle itself well into the organism when the child forms such images and works on them. Equally, everything in speech of a musical nature, rhythm, recitation and the like, help in this. Music, especially the training of memory for music, will be specially beneficial for a somewhat fanciful child. These are the methods we must use to work upon a child whose ego does not seem to want to enter his or her organism properly, and who therefore might easily remain a victim of too great enthusiasms.

When, on the other hand, we notice that children are becoming too materialistic, that the ego tends to become too dependent on the body, we need only have them draw those geometrical forms that are otherwise grasped more by thought. The moment we let the children draw geometrical forms we create the counterpoise to an excessive absorption of the ego. You will see from this that it is possible to educate properly when we use the subjects of instruction correctly. If a child—because of talent or other reasons—is receiving special musical training and we notice that they are becoming too dependent on their organism, that there is a certain heaviness in their singing, we must try to guide them to practice more spontaneous listening rather than musical memory. We can always look for a balance in these tendencies, either by helping the children to draw in their ego with the methods I have described, or by preventing the ego from becoming too drawn into the bodily organism. One of these conditions would certainly arise if we failed to maintain the right balance. It is especially good when we try to regulate things through the way we teach language. All the musical elements in language contribute to the absorption of the ego. When I notice that this happens too strongly, I take up something with the child that concerns rather the meaning and content of language. In this case I will work in such a way that I call upon the child concerning the meaning of things. In the other case, when children are becoming dreamy or fanciful, I try to make them take up more the rhythmic element of language, meter and recitation. The teacher must acquire the ability to achieve this artistically, and in so doing can develop a certain sensitive sureness.

Actually, there are whole subjects that help us when we want to protect the ego from being sucked into the organism too strongly. These are above all geography, history, and everything where the emphasis is on the picture element and on drawing. In history, for example, it is quite excellent to develop your story in such a way that it engenders vivid sympathy in the children, so that you call up in them veneration, love, or even hatred (provided the personality under discussion is contemptible). This participation of heart and soul is the important thing, and such a treatment of history can do a great deal to prevent the children from becoming too materialistic. But if through insight into child development, which we must acquire, we notice that through an overdose of this sort of history lesson the children begin to show signs of fanciful dreaminess, we must try the other things that have been described. And all this must be integrated within the curriculum. It must be started at the right age, and therefore it is good to keep our eyes on the children for years. If we see the children becoming too dreamy through the stories of history, then, when the right moment arrives, we must permeate the subject with ideas, with the great interrelationships in history. In short: individual treatment of historical events and personalities prevents the ego from being absorbed too much by the bodily organism; illuminating history with ideas that cover whole epochs stimulates the entrance of the ego into the organism.

Too much drawing and too many pictures can easily lift the ego out of the organism, with all the consequences we have described. When a child shows signs of instability as a result of drawing, painting, or perhaps even writing, the remedy is to have him or her understand the meaning of what they have done. Have them think, for instance, about the rosette they have drawn, or admire the forms of the letters of the alphabet and thus become conscious of them. While mere writing and drawing take the children out of themselves, the observation of what they have drawn or written brings them back again into themselves.

These things show us how we can use every detail correctly in our teaching when we develop it truly as an art. It is of enormous importance that we consider such things seriously. Take, for instance, the teaching of geography. On the whole it tends to prevent the ego from being drawn in too deeply, and we can employ it with good effect with a child who is in danger of becoming too materialistic; we will lead such a child to an active interest in geography. On the other hand, if the child tends to become too dreamy and romantic through lessons in geography, this can be counteracted by making him or her grasp concepts such as the differences in altitude above sea level, or by leavening the geography instruction with other kinds of thinking more closely related to geometry; that will bring the ego back into the organism.

The full value of all this will be appreciated only if we are capable of looking deeply into the wonderful structure of the human organism and its harmony with the whole universe. Just imagine what we have been observing, that the development of a child between birth and puberty is an interplay of the cosmic-sculptural forces and the cosmic-musical forces—naturally with the most diverse variations. Looking at the human constitution you will find, as we have often pointed out, on the one hand the physical body and the formative force or etheric body; these two never separate between birth and death—they belong together in a certain sense continuously from birth to death. On the other hand, physical and etheric bodies separate, in falling asleep, from the astral body—first of all, the etheric body from the astral body—and upon awaking they join together again. The etheric and astral bodies, we see, are less closely linked than are, for instance, the

physical and etheric bodies. And like the latter pair, the ego and
the astral body are closely connected and do not separate during
sleep. Well, what are human beings, then, through our physical
body here on Earth? We are beings who live in reciprocal intimacy
with the air around us. A given amount of air is at one moment
within our physical body, at the next outside it; we breathe in,
we breathe out. This breathing in and out reveals in a delicate
way the difference between our waking and sleeping conditions.
There is a subtle difference, and in matters of great importance it
is usually the subtle differences that are most significant.

What happens here through the interaction between the astral
body and etheric body takes place in our waking state and in sleep
as well. The interplay between the sculptural element and the
musical during the formative years is the continual and mutual
intervibration of the astral and the etheric bodies, in which the
ego vibrates with the astral, the etheric with the physical body.
You see, we human beings really breathe in our ego and astral
body upon awaking and breathe them out again upon falling
asleep. This is a sort of greater breathing process that we can
compare with the lesser one. Actually, every time we fall asleep
we emerge from our physical and etheric bodies and enter into a
more intimate relationship with the surrounding air, because our
ego and our astral body are then directly in the air. Awake, we
direct our breathing from within; asleep, we do it from outside,
from the soul. Consider that on the one hand the air, at least a
certain quantity of it, is at one moment within the human organism and then out of it, and on the other hand that the entire
human constitution, from the physical body to the ego, takes part
in the breathing process, and you will see why we must closely
observe the nature of this interaction between the human constitution and the air in order to understand the human being.

You have probably all studied some chemistry, and you may
recall the patience with which reasonably conscientious teachers

explained to the children or young people that air, consisting of oxygen and nitrogen, is not a genuine chemical compound but a sort of mixture. In air, then, the coexistence of oxygen and nitrogen is less than a chemical compound; it is a looser connection. How is this fact related to the human being? We find the cosmic counterpart within us, in the loose connection between the astral and etheric bodies. Were oxygen and nitrogen chemically united, the etheric and astral bodies would also be inseparably joined together, and we would never be able to go to sleep. The inner relation between the astral and etheric bodies is mirrored in the outer constitution of the air, and vice versa. The human being is organized in accord with the cosmos. Within ourselves we are a microcosm, although certain things that in the outer world are ordered in a physical way in us are of a soul nature. Outside in nature we are concerned with physical laws governing oxygen and nitrogen; within us, with the laws of soul active in the relationship of the etheric and astral bodies. When we look at human beings and what happens within our organism—a scientist of the spirit can observe this—we realize that when we breathe we have in the marvelous vibrations, which we can describe as vibrations of light, a swift intermingling of astral and etheric vibrations; this is an inner process of inhaling and exhaling. On the other hand, we see the same thing happening one step lower down in the physical process of out- and in- breathing. Contemplating this, we can positively see how human beings, as spirit-soul beings, are constantly freeing themselves of their physical surroundings, just as in a mixture the heavier parts become dislodged and fall to the bottom while the lighter ones remain on top. Such processes take place in many different forms in the human being. But we must find them, as it were, among the things we observe, perceive, and take into ourselves in order that we may understand them, and then, in meditative remembering, as I explained yesterday, transform them into artistic education.

There is something more that we must consider. What is it that carries our ego into the physical world at birth when we descend from the spiritual world? It is our head. The head is, so to speak, the carriage in which the ego journeys into the physical world, and when it arrives it transforms its whole condition of life at this transition from the spiritual to the physical world. Paradoxical as it may seem to one who looks at things externally, it is so that in the spiritual world, before we prepare to be born here on Earth, we are in a constant state of motion. There movement is our true element. Should we wish to continue this movement, we would never be able to enter the physical world; we are saved from this contingency through the head organism, which adapts itself to the rest of the organism. In a sense, then, our head becomes the chariot we ride into the physical world, but when it arrives it comes to a halt and rests comfortably upon the rest of the body. Even when the rest of the body walks, the head does not join in; just as persons who ride in a carriage or in a train are themselves at rest, the ego, which before birth was in constant motion, comes to rest once it has descended to Earth; it ceases to carry out its former movements. This points to something of extraordinary significance.

When modern embryologists study the development of the human embryo in the mother's womb, they observe that at first the head is large and definitely shaped in comparison to the other amorphous members that take shape later, yet they proceed to assume that all the phenomena are of uniform importance. In this respect modern embryology is really rather limited—so much so, in fact, that it is difficult to find common ground for discussion with present-day physiologists. Their thinking works on an entirely different plane. What matters is that fertilization acts primarily upon the limb-nature of the human being, upon parts other than the head. Essentially the head receives its configuration from the whole cosmos, not from the father. The human head is in fact not conceived from the male parent but out of the cosmos. Furthermore, the head as potentiality already exists in the unfertilized human cell, in which the head—while still under a cosmic influence—is affected by the fact that fertilization acts first upon the rest of the organism. Not until the embryo begins to develop do the effects of the embryonic development work back upon the head. Thus we can discover even by studying embryonic development quite externally, but by really studying it, that the head forms itself out of the mother's body before any direct influence by fertilizing forces has been exerted. It is just like building a carriage in a workshop, a carriage that is then to carry a passenger; they come toward each other. In the same way the head is prepared in order to receive into itself the descending human ego. And for a long time after birth, really through all the formative years, a human being bears traces of this confluence of the human and the cosmic organizations.

When the spirit of the education we want to nurture here has entered the teacher—I should like to say as a genuine soul habit—a result will be that teachers facing a class will be enormously fascinated by what takes place in the individual children. Even between the seventh and fourteenth years—certainly perceptible only to intimate observation—a distinct differentiation can be made between a certain withdrawal or retreat of a superhuman organization from the head and a permeation of the head with forces streaming up and pouring in from the rest of the organism. You must think all of this over in conjunction with what I said in the first two lectures, because one thing has to be balanced by the other.

It must always be interesting for the teacher to study the difference between the sculptural form of the child's head and the structure of the rest of the organism, but one must look at the two phenomena in different ways. If you want to consider the changes that take place in the head you must bring yourself to be a sculptor; but to consider the changes in the rest of the organism, you must bring yourself to be a musician imbued with eurythmy. As for the latter, there is no point in observing how the fingers grow, for example, but one should note any changes in the kind of motions the children make. That indeed reacts back upon the shaping of the organism, though not through the structural but through the dynamic elements. If someone has excessively long arms or legs, these will be heavier than normal. It is not their form that has a distinct effect, but rather the force of weight that they work with, and it is this weight that mingles with the musical forming of the movements. If we want to form a correct judgment of someone whose arms and legs are so long that they don't know what to do with them, we must approach such a person with a judgment alive to music, with an intimate judgment filled with life; we must feel how the child's legs keep crossing and recrossing because they are too long and keep getting into each other's way, and therefore the motion is abnormal. Or the arms never know what they are meant to do because of their excessive weight. How wonderful it is to think that through spiritual science one gets to know the human being so intimately by applying such knowledge! One will then no longer observe matters from the standpoint of the emotions as one had considered them before. When we see someone with small hands and arms, we will immediately say to ourselves: well, there's no great urge in that person to hit someone. But when arms and hands are too long and heavy, the impulse to hit out must be charged to that person's karma, their destiny, and not judged from an emotional point of view.

Keeping such things in mind brings us much closer to one another, especially to those who are still developing, for we will discover a remarkable secret. Out of this person's bodily form—as you will be able to say when you study it as we have—I can determine how he or she has developed and the whole composition of his or her soul. I find the significance of a certain shape of head, a certain weight of arms and legs, and so forth. Whether someone steps delicately along on tiptoe or—like Fichte, whose complete figure bore witness to the fact—walks firmly, setting down his heels, tells us an immense amount and gives us the feeling that we are learning to know human beings much better. Of course, these things do not reveal any personal or intimate secrets; they are experiences we have with others in a human and social interaction that become more intimate between teacher and child during instruction. A feeling can also arise that whenever we meet someone there is something to learn about them when we see them face to face, and something else when we see them from the back. We should let life itself engrave in us our understanding of the nature of life. For example, a student of Fichte's who understood life correctly would have looked at Fichte from the front during his lectures in order to take in what he said; however, in order to get to know Fichte's character he would have had to look at him from behind, for this would disclose his whole manner and build. The formation of the back of his head, his back and hunched shoulders, the way he moved his hands and carried his head, all this fairly challenged the observer to see in Fichte precisely the personality he was in the world.

Remarkable things come to light if you get to know children in this way; that is, if you are the sort of teacher who is inclined toward an understanding directed to matters of destiny and not the sort who gets angry at emotional children, continually nags at them to sit still and be quiet, and finally throws the inkpot at them, saying: "I'll teach you how to be quiet!" This is a rather drastic way to put it, but even if the reaction were less radical we teachers and educators must recognize it as wrong.

If we can get away from such behavior and direct our anthroposophical study of the human being more toward children's bodily form so that their organism tells us something of their soul nature, we may come to know that we are treating them differently from the usual way. And wonder of wonders! By approaching the children like this we learn to love them, and we shall gradually understand them with greater and greater love. In just this way we shall gain a powerful feeling of support for teaching and educating the child lovingly. These are the ways we acquire the right feelings and attitudes as educators and teachers. It would be a mistake to believe, for instance, that one could become a composer by studying a textbook on music theory, or learn to paint from a book on aesthetics. A person doesn't become a painter like that, but rather by learning to use color, by acquiring the necessary skill in handling color, and so forth. To become a sculptor one must learn to understand the forms of an organism, and this is intensely interesting in the art of sculpture or elsewhere. As a sculptor you will have quite a different feeling when modeling a head from the feeling you have when forming the rest of the organism. When working on the head you will constantly have the feeling that the head is working on you from within so that you must retreat from it, that something coming out of it is pressing against you. In modeling the rest of the organism, on the other hand, you feel that you are pressing in, while this section of the organism is withdrawing from you. So your feelings are exactly opposite in modeling the head and modeling the rest of the body, and this shows how necessary it is to learn the appropriate approach in every single case.

The same holds true in the field of education. If you expected to glean how a class should be handled from a textbook on education, it would be exactly the same as trying to become a painter by means of a textbook on aesthetics. Nothing will come of it. But if you put into practice the anthroposophical knowledge of the human being as we are doing here, the talent for education will take hold of you. Many more people have this potential talent than you would imagine. Following this first step you will acquire certain other qualities that every good teacher needs. There is no subject on which more nonsense is talked today than education, although so many people take an extraordinary interest in it; one finds such talk particularly distressing because it affects the next generation. But especially in education as in so many other fields, popular slogans can be confronted by a deeper grasp of human nature. We can understand well-meaning laypeople saying that instruction must be a pleasure for the children, but even teachers use the phrase, and it should be strictly discredited when passed on by professionals! If you consider how it is in reality, you must ask: how should a teacher go about making the children radiantly happy when there are particularly difficult things for the children to overcome? Or think about what children are like and realize that they have to be in school from morning till night: how will you contrive to give them nothing but pleasure and then more pleasure? It simply cannot be done. It is one of those phrases coined by people who have no contact with reality.

The simple fact is that certain things give children no pleasure and yet they must be done. For one thing, if teachers were to give children nothing but pleasure, the children would be unable to develop a feeling for duty, for this can only be achieved if we learn to overcome ourselves. So it is not a question of "nothing but pleasure," but of gaining the children's love through the art of our educating, so that under our guidance they will do things they dislike doing or even things that make them suffer a bit. Bring love to your teaching, and if you succeed in awakening the right kind of love in the children something besides joy will develop in them. Loyal affection and devotion to the teacher will grow in the children so that they come to feel: there are many difficult things we must do, but for that teacher I will do the hard things.

You see that in looking at teaching and educating we have arrived at a different method of working from what is commonly thought to be pedagogical. What we have discussed here will show you that we can overcome many of the difficulties in the classroom by coming to understand how to create the right relationship between teacher and pupil.

PART TWO

Deeper Insights into Education

Preface

IN considering the beginnings of Waldorf education—now a movement of over 900 schools worldwide—one may well be astonished to find that Rudolf Steiner preferred to convey its revolutionary thrust by word of mouth rather than by means of the printed page. Over a period of almost six years (1919–1924) Steiner, traveling widely in Germany, Switzerland, France, Norway, Holland, and England, gave some 200 lectures on the Waldorf approach, speaking to small groups of qualified teachers as well as to large public audiences.

Important seeds had been planted in Steiner's early years through his own experiences as tutor and teacher. In 1907 he formulated his views on education in an essay entitled "The Education of the Child in the Light of Anthroposophy."[9] It was not until twelve years later, soon after the First World War, which left Middle Europe shattered, morally depleted, and financially in ruins, that Steiner answered the call from Emil Molt, the owner of the Waldorf Astoria cigarette factory in Stuttgart, to found a school initially intended for the children of the factory workers.

Three mighty courses of fourteen lectures each (*Foundations of Human Experience,* also called *Study of Man; Practical Advice to Teachers; Discussions with Teachers*) given over a period of two

---

9. See *The Education of the Child and Early Lectures on Education*, Anthroposophic Press, Great Barrington, MA, 1996.

weeks (August–September 1919) to a group of twelve young, able, enthusiastic teachers, launched the bold venture that was to grow into a strong movement with schools in Europe, North America, South America, Africa, Asia, Australia, and New Zealand. Steiner became the director of the Waldorf School in Stuttgart. He was tireless in giving his time and strength, entering into every detail of the curriculum, the work in the classroom, the life of the students; he counseled teachers, visited classes, and advised parents, all this in spite of a host of other commitments in such fields as medicine, agriculture, and social renewal.

In studying Rudolf Steiner's educational work, a careful distinction should be made between the courses given to the first teachers of the Waldorf School in Stuttgart, who were well prepared through a sound basis in anthroposophy, and those given to public audiences that often had not the slightest background in spiritual science.

Steiner emphasized that the Waldorf approach was a great deal more than the application of teaching methods; this new art of education was born out of a solid anthroposophical foundation, out of a knowledge of the growing child as a being of body, soul, and spirit. Today it would be said that Waldorf education is holistic, that it aims at unfolding the capacities of hand, heart, and head in the child according to the stages of child development.

The three lectures published here were given in 1923 to the original teachers of the Waldorf School, who had received four years of intensive training and practice under Steiner's personal guidance. They should be read with this background in mind; their original and sometimes startling message will then be understood more readily. For beginners, it may well be advisable first to work through Steiner's written work and some of the earlier public lectures, for example, *A Modern Art of Education*, fourteen lectures delivered in August 1923 in Ilkley, England; or *The Renewal of Education*, fourteen lectures given to Swiss teachers in April and May 1920 in Basel, Switzerland; or *The Spiritual Ground of Education*, four lectures given at Manchester College, Oxford, England, in August 1922. It should be mentioned that many invaluable indications on education will also be found in Steiner's lectures on the social question, the arts, medicine, curative education, and the sciences.

Serious readers will readily become aware that Steiner's comprehensive teachings are undogmatic in character. They are indications, seeds that parents, teachers, or anyone genuinely interested in children's development and well-being can make their own and verify through experience. Rather than encountering a number of easily applicable educational recipes, they will find themselves engaged in a process of discovery in the realm of childhood and adolescence.

René M. Querido

1

Gymnast, Rhetorician, Professor:
A Living Synthesis

THE impressions I have gathered here in the school have prompted me to use the short time I can be with you to say something that emerges directly out of these impressions. After all, the fruitfulness of our activity in an institution like the Waldorf School depends, as does indeed the art of education as a whole, on the ability of the teachers to develop the attitude that will enable them to carry through their work with assurance and be active in the right way. On this occasion, therefore, I would like to speak in particular about the teachers themselves. I would like to preface what I have to say with some brief remarks I made recently in a course for teachers in England, though from a somewhat different point of view. I shall then add a few things that will enable you, if you let them work in the right way on your souls, to develop this right attitude more and more. The question of attitude, or mood of soul, is very much connected with the art of education. You may possess an admirable mastery of the principles of teaching, you may be able to work them out with intelligence and feeling, but what we are trying to do will fall on fertile soil only if the general attitude that we take with us into the school can be made into a harmonious whole.

We humans are threefold beings not only from the many standpoints we have often discussed but also from those that lie a little closer to the earthly than do the higher, spiritual perspectives.

This threefoldness reveals itself quite specifically if we focus on the way human beings have developed their education. We need not go back very far; indeed, if we went back to very ancient times our view would have to alter somewhat. We need only go back to the Greek era in human evolution, to a period that still stirs the minds of those in our Western civilization. At that period we find that the educator was really a gymnast, intent above all upon molding pupils into maturity through the outer, physical, bodily nature. However, we shall not properly understand the Greek gymnasts, especially the earlier ones, unless we realize that they were quite as much concerned with the development of the soul and spirit as of the body. It is true that the Greeks laid stress upon physical exercises, which were all formed in an artistic sense, as the means of bringing pupils to maturity. What is so little realized nowadays, however, is that these exercises, whether dance movements or some other rhythmical or gymnastic movements, were devised in such a way that through the unfolding and expression of rhythm, measure, and the like, spiritual beings were able to draw near, beings who lived in the movements, in the rhythm and measure in which the pupils were trained. While the pupils were doing something with their arms and legs, a spiritual influence passed from the limb system, including the metabolic system, into the rhythmic and the nerve-sense systems; in this way the whole human being was developed. Thus, one should not say that in Greece primary importance was attached to the cultivation of gymnastics, for this gives the impression that these exercises were cultivated then as they are nowadays, that is, mostly in an entirely outward and physical way. In fact, with the Greeks gymnastics also included the education of soul and spirit. The Greek educator was a gymnast; he educated the body, and along with the body the soul and spirit, because he had the capacity, as if by magic, to draw down the world of soul and spirit into bodily movements. The more ancient Greek gymnasts were perfectly conscious of this. They had no desire to educate human beings in an abstract, intellectual way or to teach their pupils as we do today. We speak exclusively to the head, even if we do not intend to. The Greeks brought their pupils into movement; they brought them into movement that was in harmony with the dynamic of the spiritual and physical cosmos.

In following the course of human evolution, we find that among the Romans the art of cultivating the soul and spirit by way of the bodily nature had been forgotten. They approached the soul directly, and education took place especially through the medium of *speech*, the faculty lying nearest to the soul element in ordinary life. Roman education did, in fact, draw forth from speech what was to form the pupils; the educator thus ceased to be a gymnast and became a rhetorician. Beautiful speech was from Roman times onward the essential element in education, and actually remained so throughout the Middle Ages. Beautiful speech—in forming words and in the consciousness that the word is being sculpturally and musically formed—has its effect on the whole human being. The most important principles of education were derived from this consciousness. The Greeks had gone right back to the bodily foundation of the human being, and from there drew everything into the realm of soul and spirit. The Romans concerned themselves with the middle part of the human being, with the sublimated expression of the rhythmic system, with the musical speech of poetry. They trusted that if speech were handled properly, this musical and sculptural-painterly speech would work downward into the bodily and upward into the spiritual. Intellectual training also played no part in this form of education; special importance was instead attached to speaking.

Then, from the fifteenth century onward, the rhetorician as educator was gradually superseded by the professor [*Doktor*[10]].

---

10. The German *Doktor* does not refer to a medical doctor in this context, but to a scholar with a doctoral degree.

Even teachers who have only passed through a training college nowadays are in this sense really "professors." Hitherto there was some justification for this, if indeed the ideal of the professor was not held as it once was by a gymnastics teacher I knew well. He felt extremely uncomfortable on any gymnastic apparatus but loved to get up on a platform and hold forth theoretically about gymnastics. His pupils sat crouched and bent on their benches and listened to the gymnastics lectures. This sort of thing could not have happened in any other institution, but in this training college he could get up and lecture like this once a week. He felt quite learned; he felt, in fact, like a real professor. The principle that the basis of education lies not in the rhythmic system but in the head, in the nerve-sense system, became more and more prominent as humanity evolved from the fifteenth century into the modern age. Hence it is not so easy today for teachers in the Waldorf School to adhere to the principle that they should have no desire to realize this ideal of the learned professor. I do not mean this outwardly but inwardly. It is not easy, because it is a normal part of modern consciousness to believe that something is gained by becoming "learned." In our civilization, however, a healthy condition will be achieved only when we realize that to be "learned" in this sense is actually harmful—and that far from adding anything to a human being, it takes something away. Though I am always delighted when someone nods intelligent assent to the sort of thing I have been speaking about, I am also a little uncomfortable about the nodding, because people take the matter much too lightly. There is little inward inclination to lay aside the doctorate, even if one does not have it oneself, even if one only carries the attitude in one's general consciousness. Furthermore, the trend that has caused the earlier gymnast and rhetorician to be superseded by the professor is so much part and parcel of modern civilization that it cannot easily be eradicated. It is in education, of course, that we notice most clearly the unfortunate effects upon a person who has gone through a doctoral training; yet what has put the professor into a leading position in education has been necessary for the entire development of intellectualism in modern culture.

We have reached a point when we must cultivate the synthesis of these three elements, for this division into gymnast, rhetorician, and professor is yet another example of the threefoldness of human nature, and it is above all in the realm of education that this synthesis should be achieved. If we could manage things ideally, the teacher should cultivate gymnastics in the noblest sense, rhetoric in the noblest sense—with all that was associated with it in ancient times—and also the professorial element in the noblest sense. Then these three elements should be integrated into a whole. I almost shudder at having to describe so dryly what you must know in this regard and must receive in your hearts' minds [*die Gesinnung*], because I'm afraid it may again get distorted, as happens with so much that must be said. It must not be distorted. Teachers should simply realize that for their own art of education they need a synthesis of the spiritualized gymnast, the ensouled rhetorician, and the living, evolving spiritual element [*das Geistige*], not the dead and abstract spiritual element.

The whole faculty ought to work together to assimilate these things, to develop gymnastics in the noblest sense and also what we have in eurythmy. If you really succeed in penetrating eurythmy inwardly, you will experience for yourselves that there is an active element of soul and spirit in every eurythmic movement. Every eurythmic movement calls forth an element of soul from the deepest foundations of the human being, and every gymnastic movement, if rightly executed, calls forth in us a spiritual atmosphere into which the spiritual element can penetrate livingly, not in a dead, abstract way.

The rhetorical element, in the noblest sense of the word, still has a particular significance for the teacher today. No educators, in whatever sphere of education they may be engaged, should fail to do their utmost to have their own speaking approach as closely as possible an artistic ideal. The need for cultivating speech as such should always be kept in mind. This is something that has vanished so completely from human consciousness that in this age of intellectualism professors of rhetoric are appointed at universities mainly out of an old habit.

Curtius was a professor of rhetoric at Berlin University, but he was not allowed to lecture on the subject because lectures on the art of speech were felt to be superfluous at a place of higher education. He therefore had to discharge his duty in other ways than by lecturing about rhetoric, though in his official appointment he still bore the title of professor of rhetoric. This shows how we have ceased to attach any real value to the art of speech; this is connected with our ever increasing disregard for the artistic element as such. Today we usually think because we do not know what else to do, and that is why we have so few real thoughts. The thoughts produced in the style of our modern thinking are the worst possible. The best are those that rise up out of an individual's humanness while he or she is engaged in some kind of action. Good thoughts are those that evolve out of beautifully formulated speech—when, out of such beautifully formulated speaking, thoughts rebound in us. Then something from the archangel lives in our thinking through the speech, and it is far more significant that we be able to listen to this speech than that we develop prosaic human thinking, however cleverly we might do so. This can be achieved, however, only if we, especially those engaged in education, clearly realize how remote modern thinking is from reality, from the world. We have, of course, produced a splendid science, but the sad thing is that this science really knows nothing; and because it knows nothing, it is driving the very life out of human culture and civilization. We need not turn into revolutionaries because of this, or go about shouting such things indiscriminately in the world; what we need is to work out of this consciousness in the school.

Not only has thinking gradually become more and more abstract, but so has everything that relates to the content of the human soul. At most, people are still aware that our highest soul faculties originate in sudden flashes [*einfällen*], and are especially proud when something occurs to them [*einfällt*] in this way. Since people experience what may be the most valuable element in their soul as something severed from the universe, they become inwardly barren and lifeless, alienated from reality. Our musicians compose music, they write melodies and harmonies, because these happen to occur to them. Certainly one might think it quite a good thing if such things occur to someone frequently in the realm of music; but why do they occur to them? Why should some melody suddenly occur to them out of nothingness? There appears to be neither a human or cosmic reason that a melody should occur suddenly to an individual who was born in and lives in this or that time or place. Why? There is only meaning in it when one has a connection with the cosmos in experiencing a melody, when one experiences the connection with the cosmos in experiencing a melody. One need not sail away into symbolism, but the connection with the cosmos must be experienced. The melody must really be "spoken" into us by the spirit of the world; then it has meaning and does something to promote progress in the world.

A great deal of ahrimanic influence can be found in the world today; indeed, the evolution of the world would be impossible without it. One of the worst instances of the ahrimanic, however, is that in order to become a qualified professor one must write a thesis. There is no real connection between writing a thesis and becoming a professor; the only connection is purely external, ahrimanized. Such things are taken seriously in our civilization today, however, and force their way into education, because educational institutions exert their influence from above downward, and the whole mode of their organization is totally unsound. Merely to say this sort of thing gets us nowhere, except to make us unpopular and create enemies for ourselves. In working here, however, we should be fully awake to the fact that we are called to work out of different premises.

Nowadays, for example, in lectures on the physiology of nutrition, we would be told that potatoes—carbohydrates—contain so much carbon, so much oxygen, and so on; that protein contains so and so much carbon, hydrogen, oxygen, and nitrogen; fats, so and so much nitrogen, and so on; that the various "salts" we consume are composed of what nowadays are called the chemical elements; and finally, that the amounts of carbon, oxygen, nitrogen, and so forth that we need can be calculated. Thus is adduced the modern theory of nutrition. It is exactly as though someone who wanted to know how a watch comes into existence were first to ascertain how gold is produced up to the moment when it is delivered to the watchmaker, or how the glass for the watch is produced, and so on. Such a person insists on getting to know the parts but never on knowing what the watchmaker does with them. In all eternity such a person will never really know anything about the watch. He or she may be well informed about the glass, the hands, and the materials comprising the watch, but knows nothing about the watch itself. The same sort of thing is true regarding human nutrition if people limit themselves to the knowledge that fats are constituted of such and such chemical elements, carbohydrates of others, and so forth. We begin to know something about nutrition only if we can enter in a living way into the fact that what we eat in a potato, for example, is related to the root. If we eat something related to the root it is quite different from consuming in flour something that is related to the *seed*, as in corn or wheat. What really matters is not how much carbohydrate there is in a potato or a kernel of corn. Rather, if I prepare a foodstuff from seeds, from corn, this foodstuff has to be digested in the area of the human being that extends to the lymph vessels, and reaches the nerve-sense system in a condition such that it can provide the foundation for thinking. When I eat a potato, which is related to the root, it is not the human digestive tract or the lymphatic system that reduces the potato to a state where the body can assimilate it. No, here the midbrain is required, and when we eat potatoes the task of digestion is imposed upon the midbrain. When we eat a different kind of food this burden is not present. If we eat potatoes in excess, we impose upon the midbrain the task of the primary digestion; that is to say, we undermine the real function of the midbrain in relation to the nerve-sense system, which is to permeate thoughts with feeling [*Gemüt*]. We thus thrust our thinking into the forebrain, where it becomes intellectual and to some extent actually animal-like.

The essential point is not whether a potato, or cabbage, or corn, is composed of such and such a percentage of carbohydrates. For a true physiology of nutrition all that is irrelevant. What we really need to know is how these things actually work within the human being. If we wish to develop a living grasp of what the human being needs today, we must free ourselves from all these things that can never give us true knowledge. The way we talk about nature nowadays is not only misleading—it leads us straight into emptiness of thought, emptiness of feeling.

Now you are all aware that there is a well-known process in the human being by means of which carbon combines with oxygen so that carbon dioxide is produced, that is, the mixture of carbon and oxygen that we exhale. You will often hear this process talked about as if it were a sort of inner burning, the same sort of thing as when a candle burns. There, too, carbon combines with oxygen, but to talk in this way is about as intelligent as to ask why the human being needs two lungs; we might just as well substitute two stones, two inorganic objects. If we mentally transfer into the human being the outer process of burning, we think in the same way we would if we viewed the lungs as two stones. The burning that takes place outwardly in connection with oxygen is a dead burning, an inorganic burning; what takes place in the human being is a living burning, permeated with soul. Any process that takes place outside in nature changes when it occurs in the human being; in the human being it is permeated with soul; it is spiritual. What carbon and oxygen do together within the human organism bears the same relation to what happens outside as the living lungs bear to two stones. It is more important to guide one's whole life of feeling in this direction than to ponder these things; then in all realms of soul life one would come to a direct experience of nature that could truly guide one from nature to the human being. Nowadays people remain outside with nature and do not reach the human being at all.

You will discover that if you speak to children with this kind of feeling and attitude [*Gesinnung*] they will understand the most difficult things as they need to be understood at their particular ages. If you rely on the accursed textbooks that are so popular, the children really understand nothing; you torment the children, bore them, call forth their scorn. What you must do is create a personal relationship to the world that is both living and true to reality. That, above all, is what the teacher needs. I would like to emphasize strongly at the beginning that teachers should continually strive to bring to life in themselves what has become dead in the course of civilization. One of the chief tasks in Waldorf education is to bring life to knowledge, and to feel a kind of repugnance for the way things are presented nowadays in so-called scientific textbooks. After having conquered this stage of repugnance we should be able to develop what really lives within us and passes over to the children in a living way. We must begin at this point with ourselves and then look at nature like this. A good deal of courage is needed, because much of what is true is regarded nowadays as sheer madness. Everything possible should be done to develop this courage.

Think of a butterfly. It lays an egg, the caterpillar crawls out and spins its cocoon, becoming a chrysalis, and finally the butterfly flies out of the chrysalis. These things are described in the textbooks, but how? Without any consciousness whatever of the wonderful mystery that really lies here. The butterfly lays an egg, but it is essential that this egg be laid at the proper time of year and that it be receptive to everything that works as the earthy, as the solid or solid-fluid quality in nature. The most essential thing for the development of the egg is the "salty" element. Then comes the time when in addition to the earthy element, the fluid—and with the fluid the etheric—takes over. The fluid element, which becomes permeated with the etheric, passes over into the development of the caterpillar that crawls out of the egg. When we have the egg, we think primarily of the earth with the physical element. When we have the caterpillar that crawls out of the egg we see its shape. What crawls out is a being actually permeated with the etheric, fluid-watery element, and that is what makes the caterpillar into a caterpillar.

Now the caterpillar must develop its being in the air; the most important thing now for the caterpillar is that it come in contact with the light, so that it actually lives in the light-permeated air but at the same time expresses an inner relationship to the astral element, and with this relationship to astrality, absorbs light. It is essential for the caterpillar to be exposed through its sensory system to the rays of the sun, to the radiating sun with its light. Next you see in the caterpillar what can be perceived in its most extreme form when you lie in bed with the lights still burning, and moths fly toward the light. There you have the apparently inexplicable urge of the moth to sacrifice itself. We shall hear why. The moth dashes into the light and is burnt up. Caterpillars have the same urge regarding the radiating light, but they are organized in such a way that they cannot hurl themselves into the sun. The moth can hurl itself into the light. The caterpillar has the same urge to give itself up to the light but cannot do so, for the sun is a long way off. The caterpillar develops this urge, goes out of itself, passes into the radiating light, gives itself up, spinning physical material out of its own body into the rays of the sun. The caterpillar sacrifices itself to the rays of the sun; it wishes to destroy itself, but all destruction is birth. It spins its sheath during the day in the direction of the sun's rays and when it rests at night what has been spun hardens, so that these threads are spun rhythmically, day and night. These threads the caterpillar spins are materialized, spun light.

Out of the threads that the light has formed, that it has materialized, the caterpillar spins its chrysalis; it passes wholly into the light. The light itself is the cause of the spinning of the chrysalis. The caterpillar cannot hurl itself into the light but gives itself up to it, creating the chamber in which the light is enclosed. The chrysalis is created from above downward in accordance with the laws of form of the primal wisdom. The butterfly is formed after the caterpillar has prepared the secluded chamber for the light. There you have the whole process from the egg to the brilliantly colored butterfly, which is born out of the light, as all colors are born out of the light. The whole process is born out of the cosmos.

If the process that we see extended into a fourfoldness—egg, caterpillar, chrysalis, butterfly—is in any way condensed, then the whole is changed. When the process occurs inwardly within the animal element, what remains is a being created out of the light. You see, the only way we can really get to the essence of the matter is to picture [*vorstellen*] the process artistically. It is impossible to picture this process whereby the butterfly forms itself from the chrysalis and is born out of the light unless we picture it artistically. If you picture the process in accordance with reality, you will find yourselves in a world of wonderful artistry. Just try for yourselves and see how entirely different your consciousness is if you know something in this way. It is a consciousness entirely different from what you experience if you know something in the modern, outer way, which really gives no knowledge at all. Every detail becomes interesting if you allow yourselves, with soul and body, to grow together with the cosmos in its work of artistic creation.

Again, look at a tadpole with its resemblance to a fish; it breathes with gills and has a fishlike tail to swim with. The creature lives wholly in the watery element, the watery-earthly element. Then the tadpole develops into a frog. What happens? The blood vessels leading into the gills wither away, and the whole blood system is rounded off inwardly. Through this rounding off, the lung arises. The veins leading to the fishlike tail also wither away, but others elongate into legs so that the frog can hop about on land. This wonderful transformation of a system of blood vessels that at first feeds the gills and tail, this extraordinarily artistic transformation into lungs and limbs, is a truly marvelous process. How is it brought about? The first system of blood vessels, which feeds the gills and tail, is produced by the earthly-watery element; the second is produced by the watery-airy element that is permeated glitteringly with light.

You can learn to understand how the elements work together, but work together in an artistic way. If you reach this sort of understanding of the natural world you simply cannot help feeling as if you possessed the creative powers within yourselves. You cannot possibly be like most people nowadays when they study modern science. They are really not fully human. They just sit with their heads unhappily in their hands and strain their brains; study exhausts them. This is all unnatural; it is really nonsensical. It is just as if eating were to make us tired—but that happens only when we eat too much. Surely it is impossible to be wearied by anything that is so intimately bound up with the human being as this living-together of nature, spirit, and soul. Yet I have known many people who have been keen students, have written books, but have suffered from anemia of the brain. It is really the same as when a person suffers from anemia in some other part of the organism. No one can suffer from anemia of the brain who sees things in the way I have described, in their true relation to reality. This is something that brings us to life inwardly, which is what we need above all else in our work as teachers. We must relate ourselves directly to life, and anything we are going to introduce in our teaching should sustain and uphold us inwardly, should truly enliven us. This is why no true teaching can ever be boring. How could it be? One might as well expect children to find eating and drinking boring, which usually does not happen unless a child is ill. If our teaching is boring there must be something wrong with it, and we ought to ask ourselves in every case (unless we are dealing with a really psychopathic child) what is lacking in us when our teaching bores the children.

These are things that really matter, and we must realize, my dear friends, that we should neglect no single opportunity to quicken the inner life of soul and spirit; otherwise we cannot teach. However erudite we may be, we cannot be good teachers. This is connected with what I described as our task to bring about the synthesis of roles that in successive stages of world evolution were separate: the gymnast, the rhetorician, and the professor. It is especially necessary today that we not allow the last relics that still live in the genius of our language, which can have an effect upon our whole human nature, to vanish, but that we try to bring a musical, sculptural-painterly quality into speech so that what comes to expression in speech may again work back upon us. We should therefore make it one of the primary demands on ourselves that we never speak in a slovenly way in the school but really form and mold our speech so that as teachers our speech has something artistic about it. This may require some exertion, but it is of enormous significance. If it is achieved, there may flow out from the school an impulse for a revival, a renewal of civilization through the synthesis of gymnast, rhetorician, and professor. We must overcome the professorial quality—the learned knowledge, intellectual knowledge—that is presently the most disastrous of the three in all education. We can achieve something with children only by being human beings, not merely by being able to think.

This is the introduction I wished to give you today. I will add something in later talks about matters that fundamentally concern the teacher as a person, for the educational problem is in many ways actually a problem of those who are teachers.

2

Forces Leading to Health
and Illness in Education

I have tried to show you that by permeating our knowledge with anthroposophy it is possible to unfold a vital life of soul. We need this vital soul life if we wish to have the strength for our teaching and education. I would like to speak to you now about something that is a preeminent goal to strive for in education, namely, that through a particular orientation in educational activity, inner forces can be gathered in order to fire the heart in an educational sense.

Today I wish to speak about the following question: which forces are we really working with when we work educationally? Actually, this question cannot be answered in any definite sense by the culture of today. We can say, of course, that the outer life human beings stand within, making it possible for them to earn a living, requires them to have capacities that children cannot as yet have. We must impart such capacities to them. Proper adult behavior is perhaps also something that children cannot acquire by themselves; it must be imparted to them through education. But the answer to the question—why do we actually educate?— remains something rather superficial in modern culture because adults today don't really see anything of great value in what they became through the teaching and education they received. They don't look back with any particularly deep gratitude to what they have become through their education. Ask yourself in your own heart whether this gratitude is always alive in you. In individual cases, of course, it may be present on reflection, but on the whole we do not think with deep gratitude about our own education because the human soul [*Gemüt*] does not fully realize what education actually means, nor which forces in human nature are quickened by it. That is why it is so difficult nowadays to arouse enthusiasm for education. All our methods, all our ingenious, formed, outer methods of education, are of little value in this respect. Answers to the question—how can this or that be achieved?—are of little use. What is most important is for someone to have enthusiasm in their work, and to be able to develop this enthusiasm to the full if they are to be a true teacher. This enthusiasm is infectious, and it alone can work miracles in education. Children eagerly respond to enthusiasm, and when there is no response on their part it usually indicates a lack of enthusiasm in the teacher.

As a kind of obvious secret, let me say that although a great deal has been said about enthusiasm here, when I go through the classes in the school I see a kind of depression, a kind of heaviness in the teachers. The lessons are really conducted with a certain heaviness, and this heaviness must be eliminated. Actually, it may also express itself in artificial enthusiasm. Artificial enthusiasm can achieve nothing at all. The only enthusiasm capable of achieving anything is that which is kindled by our own living interest in the subjects we must deal with in the classroom.

Now, it is essential for you to realize that as teachers we need to develop our own consciousness; we must work at cultivating this consciousness. This effort to develop our own consciousness is certainly made infinitely more difficult by the fact that in the higher grades we must take into account the impossible demands made upon our children from outside in preparation for graduation. This lies like a leaden burden upon the teaching in the higher grades. Nevertheless, it is essential that we not lose sight of our own goal, and therefore we must work to develop this consciousness, the Waldorf teacher's consciousness, if I may so express it. This is only possible, however, when in the field of education we come to an actual experience of the spiritual. Such an experience of the spiritual is difficult for modern humanity to attain; we must both understand and face this. We must realize that we really need something quite specific, something that is hardly present anywhere else in the world, if we are to be capable of mastering the task of the Waldorf school. In all humility, without any trace of pride or arrogance, we must become conscious of this, but conscious of it inwardly, deep in our hearts, not merely by talking about it; within our hearts we must be able to become conscious of it. This is possible, however, only if we have a clear understanding of what humanity has lost in this respect, has lost just in the last three or four centuries. It is this that we must find again.

What has been lost is the realization that when human beings enter the world out of pre-earthly existence, compared with the actual forces of the human being they are beings who need to be healed. This bond of education with healing has been lost from sight. During a certain period of the Middle Ages, certainly, people believed that the human being, as man or woman on Earth, was ill and that human health had to be restored; that human beings as they existed on the earth actually stood below their proper level, and that something real had to be done in order to make men and women truly human. This is often understood merely in a formal sense. People say the human being must evolve, must be brought to a higher level, but this is meant abstractly, not concretely. It will be interpreted concretely only when the activity of education is actually brought into connection with the activity of healing. In healing someone who is sick, one knows that something has actually been achieved: if the sick person has been made healthy, he or she has been raised to a higher level, to the level of the normal human being. In ancient times, those who knew the world mysteries regarded birth as synonymous with an illness, because when human beings are born they fall in a certain sense below their proper level and are not the being they were in pre-earthly existence. In comparison with the higher human nature, it is really something abnormal for human beings to bear within them the constituents of their bodies, to have to bear a certain heaviness. It would not be considered particularly intelligent today to say that compared with the higher nature of human beings, it is of the nature of illness to have to struggle continually until death with the physical forces of the body. Without such radical conceptions, however, we cannot approach the reality of what education means. Education must have something of the process of healing. In order to make this clear, let me offer the following.

The human being really lives within four complexes of forces. In one we are active when we walk, move our legs with a pendulum swing, or when we use our legs to dance or make other movements. This movement, taking place in the outer, physical world of space, can also be pictured as bringing about changes of location in space. Similarly, other possibilities of human movement, of the arms, hands, head, eye muscles, and so forth, can be designated as changes in location of an ordinary inanimate body— that is to say, if we leave out of account the inner activity of the human being. This is one complex of forces within which the human being lives and is active.

The second is unfolded when we begin to work upon the physical substances we absorb; in the widest sense this includes everything that belongs to the activity of nourishment. Whereas the human limbs mediate what we have in common with beings that change their physical location, there is another activity we need in order to continue the activity connected with the outer substances we absorb as nourishment. If you put a piece of sugar into your mouth, it dissolves. This is a continuation of what sugar is in the outer world. Sugar is hard and white. You dissolve it, and it becomes liquid, viscous, and then undergoes further changes. The chemist speaks of chemical changes, but that is not relevant here. The sugar continually changes. It is worked upon and absorbed into the whole organism. There you have a second kind of activity. This continues right into the rhythmic system, and then the rhythmic system takes over the activity of the digestive system. What happens in this second kind of human activity, however, is very different from the human activity of moving the limbs or of moving the whole human body in the outer world. The activity of nourishment is quite different from the activity exercised when we move outwardly or, let us say, lift a weight. This activity of nourishment cannot proceed at all without the intervention, at every point of this activity, of the astral nature of the human being. The astral nature of the human being must permeate each individual part of this activity, of nourishment. In the activity that I have described as the activity of walking, grasping, and so on, we are dealing essentially with the same forces we make use of that we can also verify physically. What really happens in these movements is that the etheric organism is set in motion and through its mediation arises a leverage movement that we can see in an act of grasping or walking. If we focus on the activity of walking or grasping, we need only consider that which we have in the physical world as it is inserted within the working of the etheric; then we have what happens in the human being. We never have this, however, if we consider the activity of nourishment. This can arise only if the astral body takes hold of processes that otherwise occur in a test tube. There primarily astral forces must be at work, and no one ever considers that physical forces no longer play a part in this process. This is exceedingly interesting, because it is generally believed that in nourishment, for example, physical forces are at work. As soon as the human being no longer exists in relation to the outer world, the physical forces cease to have their *raison d'être*; they are no longer active, no longer have any effect. In the activity of nourishment, the astral and etheric forces work upon the physical substances. The physical effect of a piece of sulfur or salt outside the body has no significance within the body. The astral seizes hold only of the astral nature of a substance, and then the etheric-astral is the really active factor in nourishment.

Going further, we come to the activities that take place in the human rhythmic nature, in the blood rhythm, in the breathing rhythm. In their inner constitution these activities are similar to the forces at work in the system of nourishment. They are the result of cooperation between the etheric and the astral, but in the activity of digestion the astral is in a certain respect weaker than the etheric, and in the rhythmic activity the astral becomes stronger than the etheric. In the rhythmic system the etheric withdraws more into the background (though actually only the etheric that is *within* the human being). The etheric *outside* the human being begins to take part again in the activity exercised in the human rhythmic system, so that with the activity of breathing one actually has the force of our inner etheric body, the force of the outer ether of the world, and our human astral activity.

Now, picture to yourselves what is really going on when the human being breathes. The physical activity of carbon, oxygen, and so on is completely suppressed, but the combined working of the etheric outside, the etheric within, and the astral is a most important factor. This plays a great part. These are the forces, however, that we must know in any substance if we wish to speak of the healing effect of that substance. We cannot discover the extent to which a substance is a remedy if we do not know how that substance, when introduced into the body, is laid hold of by these three systems of forces. The whole of therapy depends upon knowledge of these three forces in connection with the substances used. Knowledge of the healing influence in the outer and inner etheric and in the astral is what constitutes therapy in the real sense. What does it mean when antimony, for example, is used as a remedy? It simply means that some form of antimony is introduced into the body; it is laid hold of in a certain way by the inner etheric forces, by the outer etheric forces that enter by way of the breathing, and by the astral forces in the human being. We realize the extent to which antimony is a remedy when we understand the effect of these three systems of forces on a substance within the human organism.[11]

In ascending to the rhythmic activity, therefore, we come to recognize a much more delicate process than exists, for example, in the activity of nourishment. It is essentially this rhythmic activity that must be considered if we wish to recognize the healing effects. Unless we know how a particular substance affects the rhythm of breathing or the blood circulation, we cannot understand the nature of this substance as a remedy.

Now the strange thing is this. Whereas the doctor brings into operation the therapeutic forces in the unconscious, in the rhythmic system of the blood circulation or the breathing, as teachers we must bring the next higher stage into operation: that which is connected with the activity in the nerves, in the senses. This is the next metamorphosis of the remedy. What we do as teachers is really to work in such a way on the physical human being that the substances that are taken up are subjected to the etheric activity and to the outer physical activity—namely, to perception, whenever something is perceived—and to the inner physical activity, that is to say, to the inner changes of location brought about mechanically through human beings moving themselves. Whereas the remedy contains the outer and inner etheric and the astral, education contains outer physical forces (as in gymnastics) and inner physical forces. When human beings bow their

---

11. Rudolf Steiner and Ita Wegman, *Extending Practical Medicine*, London, Rudolf Steiner Press, 1996.

heads, a change takes place in their entire dynamic system; the center of gravity shifts a little, and so forth. In the workings of light upon the eye we have recognized outer physical forces in their greatest delicacy and refinement. Moreover, outer physical forces are operating when pressure is made on an organ of touch. We therefore have *etheric* activity, *outer* physical forces, and *inner* physical forces—that is to say, physical changes in the nervous system, destruction in the nervous system. These are true physical processes that are actually present only in the human nervous system. As teachers, we are essentially dealing with these three systems in our work with the children. This is the higher metamorphosis of what is done in healing.

What kinds of activity are present in the human being? There are the movements of walking, grasping, the movement of the limbs, outer changes of location, the activity in the process of nourishment, the rhythmic activity—which is through and through a healing activity—and the perceiving activity, if we regard it from outside. Regarded from within, educational activity is entirely a perceiving activity.

This will now give you deeper insight into the nature of the human being. You will be able to say to yourselves: since factors are active in the rhythmic system that are healing factors, there is a doctor [*Arzt*] continually present in the human being. In fact, the whole rhythmic system is a doctor. The function of a doctor is to heal something, however, and if healing is needed there must be illness. If that is so, walking, grasping, digesting must be continual processes of illness, and breathing and blood circulation a continual healing. This is indeed the case. In modern science, however, where discrimination is lacking, no one realizes that the human being is continually becoming ill. Eating and drinking, especially, are processes that continually create illness. We cannot avoid continually injuring our health through eating and drinking. Eating and drinking to excess merely injure us more seriously, but we are always injuring ourselves to a slight degree. The rhythmic system, however, is continually healing this illness. Human life on the earth is a continual process of becoming ill and a continual healing. This process of becoming ill brings about a genuine physical illness. What the human being does in intercourse with the outer world, the consequences of walking, grasping, and the like, is a more intense but less noticeable process of becoming ill. We must counter it through a higher process of healing, through a process of education, which is a metamorphosis of the healing process.

The forces inherent in education are metamorphoses of therapeutic forces: they are therapeutic forces transformed. The goal of all our educational thinking must be to transform this thinking so as to rise fruitfully from the level of physical thinking to spiritual thinking. In physical thinking we have two categories that, in our academic age, give rise to a barren enthusiasm that has such a terrible influence. We have only two concepts: right-wrong, true-false. To discover whether something is "true" or "false" is the highest ideal of those whose entire lives are given up to the world of academia. In the concepts "true" and "false," however, there is so little reality. They are something formal, established by mere logic, which actually does nothing but combine and separate. The concepts "true" and "false" are dreadfully barren, prosaic, and formal. The moment we rise to the truths of the spiritual world we can no longer speak of "true" and "false," for in the spiritual world that would be as nonsensical as saying that to drink such and such a quantity of wine every day is "false." The expression "false" is out of place here. One says something real regarding this only by saying that such a thing gives rise to illness. Correct or incorrect are outer, formal concepts, even regarding the physical. Pertaining to the spiritual world, the concepts of "true" and "false" should be discarded altogether. As soon as we reach the spiritual world we must substitute "healthy" and "ill" for "true" and "false." If someone said about a lecture such as the one I gave here yesterday evening that it was "right," it would mean nothing at all. In the physical world things can be "right"; in the spiritual world nothing is "wrong" or "right." There, things are reality. After all, is a hunchback "true" or "false"? In such a case we cannot speak of right or wrong. A drawing may be false or correct, but not a plant; a plant, however, can be healthy or diseased. In the spiritual world things are either healthy or ill, fruitful or unfruitful. In what one does there must be reality. If someone considers that a lecture such as I gave yesterday is healthy or health-bringing, that is to the point. If they simply consider it "right," they merely show that they cannot rise to the level where reality lies. It is a question of health or illness when we are dealing with spiritual truths, and it is precisely this that we must learn in connection with education. We must learn to regard things in their educational application as either healthy or unhealthy, injurious to health. This is of particular significance if one wishes to engender a true consciousness of oneself as a teacher. It may be said that engendering this consciousness begins with passing from the "true" and "false" of logic to the reality of "healthy" or "ill." Then we come quite close to understanding the principle of healing. This can be developed in concrete detail, but we must also let ourselves be stimulated by a comprehensive knowledge of the human being, a knowledge of human beings in relation to the world around them.

When modern science describes the breathing process, for example, no particular weight is laid on the essential factor, on the actual human factor. It is said that the air consists of oxygen and nitrogen, leaving aside for the moment the other constituents. We inhale oxygen along with a certain amount of nitrogen. We then exhale oxygen combined with carbon, and also nitrogen. The percentages are measured and then people believe that the essentials of the process have been described. Little account is taken, however, of the essentially human factor. This begins to dawn upon us when we consider the following. There is a definite percentage of nitrogen in the air that is good for breathing, and also a definite percentage of oxygen. Suppose a number of people come to a region where the air is poor in nitrogen, containing less than the normal percentage. If they breathe in this nitrogen-poor air, this air gradually becomes richer in nitrogen through their breathing. They exhale nitrogen that they would not otherwise exhale in order to augment the nitrogen content of the air in the environment. I do not know whether any account is taken of this in physiology today. I have often pointed out that human beings living in air that is poor in nitrogen correct this lack; they prefer to take nitrogen from their own organic substances, depriving themselves of it in order to augment the nitrogen content of the outside air. They do the same with respect to the normal content of oxygen in the air. Human beings are so intimately related to their environment that the moment the environment is not as it ought to be they correct it, improve upon it. Thus we may say that human beings are constituted in such a way that they need nitrogen and oxygen not only for themselves; it is even more necessary that they have nitrogen and oxygen in certain percentages in their environment than within their own organism. Our environment is more important for our subconscious forces than the makeup of our own body. The incredibly interesting fact is that through our instincts we human beings have a far greater interest in our environment than in the makeup of their own body. This is something that can be proved by experiment, provided the experiments are arranged intelligently. It is only a question of arranging experiments in this realm. If our research institutes would only tackle such problems, what a vast amount there would be for them to do! The problems are there and are of tremendous importance. They are terribly important for education, too, for it is only now that we can ask why the human being needs an environment containing a particular amount of nitrogen and a particular amount of oxygen. We know that in the inner activity of nourishment or general growth, all kinds of combinations of substances are formed in the human being, revealing themselves in a definite way when we become a corpse. It is only in this dead form, however, that science today investigates these things.

Now the strange thing is that in the sphere of the human being that encompasses part of the rhythmic activity and part of the metabolic-limb activity, there is a tendency for an activity to unfold between carbon and nitrogen. In the sphere that extends from the rhythmic upward to the nerve-sense activity, there is a tendency to unfold an activity between carbon and oxygen. It is truly interesting, if one observes a soul-constitution not worn out by dry scholarship, to see sparkling soda water, where the carbon dioxide appears in the liquid as the result of the interplay of carbon and oxygen. If one observes these bubbles one has directly and imaginatively a view of what goes on in the course of the rhythmic breathing activity from the lung system toward the head. The bubbling effervescence in sparkling water is a picture of what, in a fine and delicate way, plays upward toward the human head. Looking at a spring of sparkling water, we can say that this activity of the rising carbon dioxide is really similar, only in a coarser form, to a continual, inward activity within the human being that rises from the lungs to the head. In the head, something must continually be stimulated by a delicate, intimate sparkling-water activity; otherwise, the human being becomes stupid or dull. If we neglect to bring this effervescence of sparkling water to a person's head, then the carbon within him or her suddenly shows an inclination for hydrogen instead of oxygen. This rises up to the brain and produces "marsh gas," such as is found in subterranean vaults, and then the human being becomes dull, drowsy, musty.

To begin with, these things confront us as inner—one would like to say—physical activities, but they are not really physical, for the production of marsh gas or carbon dioxide becomes in this case an inner spiritual life. We are not being led into materialism here but into the delicate weaving of the spiritual in matter.

Now if, in teaching languages, for example, we make the children learn too much vocabulary, if we make them memorize through an unconscious mechanization, this process can lead to the development of marsh gas in the head. If we bring as many living pictures as possible to the child, the effect is such that the breathing system lets the carbon dioxide effervesce toward the head. We therefore play a part, in fact, in something that makes for either health or illness. This shows us how as teachers we must demand a higher metamorphosis of the forces of healing. To be able to perceive these hidden relationships in the human organism kindles enthusiasm in the highest degree. We realize for the first time that the head is a remarkable vault that can be filled with either marsh gas or carbon dioxide. We feel we are standing before the deeper wellsprings of existence.

In the next lecture we shall study another activity, with which this activity must be brought into balance. This can happen, however, only when there is on the one hand the right kind of teaching in the musical sphere and, on the other, the right kind of teaching in lessons that are based upon outer perception [Anschauung], not upon the musical sphere. Thus, our teaching takes shape, and our interest is aroused in the human being before us. To this something else must be added: the feeling of responsibility. The consciousness of a Waldorf teacher should be imbued with the realization that makes him or her say in all humility: people are let loose into the educational world today as if the totally blind were sent out to paint in color. Few know what is really taking place in education. It is no wonder that a blind person has no particular enthusiasm for painting in color; no wonder there is no real enthusiasm for education in the world! The moment we enter into education in the way described, however, the whole art of our education will provide the stimulus for this enthusiasm, and we shall feel that we are in touch with the wellsprings of the world, and find the true feeling of responsibility. We realize that we can bring either health or illness. This enthusiasm on the one hand and a feeling of responsibility on the other must both arise in us.

3

A Comprehensive Knowledge of the Human Being as the Source of Imagination in the Teacher

STUTTGART — OCTOBER 16, 1923, EVENING

WHAT I wish to offer you in these lectures is intended essentially as an impulse toward the inner enrichment of the teacher's profession. I would like to add the following to what I said this afternoon. You see, we must bring our knowledge of the human being to the point where we can really know in detail what is going on in human beings during their ordinary activity in the world. I have shown you that the first form of activity we perceive in human beings is the movement of our limbs. Now we must ask: what actually moves our limbs? Which force is at work when we walk or do something with our arms? What is it? Now, the materialistic view—which conceives of a person as a piece of the cosmos consisting of blood, bones, and so on, described as a human being—will simply be that it is we ourselves who move the limbs! We are the true initiators of action! Fundamentally, there is no sense in putting it like that since we ourselves are the *object* in movement, are what is moved. If we ask who is the actual subject, who is moving the arm or the leg, then we arrive at something spiritual, certainly not material. We are forced to say that it is the spiritual itself that must bring physical forces, forces that we usually designate as physical, into action. Our leg must be moved by something spiritual just as, for example, we say that a piece of wood is moved by us from one place to another.

Here, however, we come to something remarkable that generally receives little attention, because a great illusion prevails regarding it. Our human movement is really a magical effect, because in it something is set in motion by the spirit. Our movement as a human being is in truth a magical effect, and our view of the human being is entirely incorrect if we do not associate the magical element with the movements we make. The will—that is to say, something purely spiritual—must intervene in physical activity; these are in truth magical effects. When you walk, an inner magician, something essential, is working within you. How does this happen? The fact that we are physical human beings, made up of bones, blood, and so forth, does not make us into moving human beings; at best it is able to make us inert beings, beings who lie permanently in bed. If we are to be able to move, the will must be directly active. Materialistic science simplifies things by theorizing about motor nerves and the like. That is nonsense. In actual fact we have in human movement a magical effect, a direct intervention of the spirit into the bodily movements. How is this possible? This will become clear in the following.

I pointed out to you this afternoon that as the human life process passes from the rhythmic system to the metabolic-limb system, what comes out of carbon has an affinity for what comes out of nitrogen, and a continual tendency arises in the human being to create combinations of carbon and nitrogen. This tendency exists, and we shall never become clear about the digestive process itself, and especially the excretory process, if this tendency toward the combination of carbon and nitrogen is not kept in mind. This tendency finally leads to the formation of cyanic acid. As a matter of fact, there exists from above downward in the human being a continual tendency to produce cyanic acid, or at any rate, cyanides. There is really no commonly accepted expression for what happens here.

What happens only goes so far as to just reach the point of coming into being, and then it is immediately arrested by the secretions, particularly of the gall bladder. Thus, in the lower part of the human being there is this continual tendency to create cyanide combinations that are arrested in their *status nascendi* by gall secretions. To create cyanide combinations in human beings, however, means to destroy the human being; the speediest method of destroying the human form [*Gestalt*] is to permeate it with cyanide. This tendency exists particularly in the direction of the metabolic-limb system; the human organism continually wants to create cyanide combinations, which are in turn immediately broken up. At this moment between the coming into being and the immediate dissolution of the cyanide compounds, the will lays hold of the muscular system. In the paralyzing of this process lies the possibility for the will to take hold so that human beings can move. From above downward there is always a tendency in the human being to destroy organic substance through a kind of poisoning. This is continually on the verge of beginning, and we would not be able to move, we could never achieve any freeing of the will, if this continual tendency to destroy ourselves were not present. Thus, to express it in a grotesque way, from above downward we have this continual tendency to make ourselves into ghosts and thereby to move by magical means. When considering human movement we must not limit our gaze to the physical body, but must turn to the human will, to the calling forth of spatial movements by purely magical means.

You see, therefore, every time people bring themselves into movement they are faced with the responsibility of intervening in the processes that are the actual processes of illness and death. On the other hand, we must know that this process of illness is opposed by the health-bringing process I spoke of this afternoon. For everything that occurs in the processes that take place in the lower human being there is a corresponding process above. Carbon has the tendency to form nitrogen compounds downward, but upward it has the tendency to form oxygen compounds.

Early alchemists called carbon the "stone of the wise," which is nothing other than carbon fully understood. Upward it has the tendency to form oxygen compounds, acids, or oxides. These stimulate the thoughts, and whenever we vitally occupy a child we stimulate the formation of carbon compounds and therewith the activity of thinking. Whenever we guide children into some form of action while they are thinking, we call forth a state of balance between the formation of carbonic and cyanic acids. In human life everything actually depends upon producing symmetry between these two things.

If a human being is occupied only with intellectual work, the process of the formation of carbonic acid is too strongly stimulated; the upper organism is saturated with carbonic acid. Now a proper, intelligently conducted musical education counteracts this excessive carbonic acid formation and enables the human being to again bring some activity—inner activity at least—into the carbonic acid process. By arranging a schedule so that the teaching of music, for example, is interspersed among the other subjects, we actually penetrate directly into the processes of illness and health in the human organism. I am not telling you these things today simply for the sake of the subject matter, although I believe they are among the most interesting things that could be found in physiology, for it is only in this way that we can see clearly into the living activity of the substances and forces within the human being. Processes of illness and health are continually taking place in the human organism, and everything a person does or is guided to do has its effect upon these processes. From this knowledge must be created a feeling of responsibility and a true consciousness of one's purpose as a teacher. We must realize, in all humility, the importance of our profession: that we help to orient what are in the most eminent sense cosmic processes. In fact, as teachers we are coworkers in the actual guidance of the world. It is the particular value of these things for our whole life of feeling [*Gemüt*] and for consciousness that I wish to stress today.

By fully penetrating this, every one of our actions will take on extraordinary importance. Think how often I have said that a person will completely misapprehend the whole of human evolution if he or she persists in trivial pictorial instructions [*Anschauungsunterricht*] and never attempts to introduce children to more than they can already understand. Such teachers fail to realize that a great deal of what they teach children in their eighth or ninth year will be accepted only if the children feel themselves to be in the presence of a beloved teacher, confronted by an obvious authority. For the children, the teacher should represent the whole world of truth, beauty, and goodness. What the teacher takes to be beautiful or true or good should be so for the pupil. This obvious authority, during the period between the change of teeth and puberty, must be the basis of all the teaching. Children do not always understand the things they accept under the influence of this authority, but accept them because they love the teacher. What they have accepted will then emerge in later life, say in the thirty-fifth year, and signify an essential enlivening of the whole inner being. Those who say that one should merely teach children trivial mental conceptions have no real insight into human nature, nor do they know what a vital force it is when at thirty-five a person can call up something he or she once accepted simply through love for a teacher. Now you can see the inner significance of what I have been saying. The human process that is the equilibrium between the carbon and the cyanide processes is essentially supported, made essentially more vital, by the fact that something of this condition remains deeply embedded in human nature in the same way that something that we may have accepted lovingly in our eighth or ninth year remains hidden and is understood only decades later. What occurs between receptivity and understanding, what lies directly in the soul in the process of balance between the lower and upper human being, together with the corresponding action of carbon, has enormous influence.

Of course, you cannot apply these things in detail in your approach to teaching, but you can go into the classroom supported by this knowledge and apply one aspect or another in various realms of your teaching; if one has acquired this knowledge, a definite result will follow. One can distinguish between those who have knowledge that is inwardly mobile or inwardly static. One who simply knows how diamonds, graphite, and coal appear in nature outside the human being, and goes no further than that, will not teach in a very lively way. If one knows, however, that the carbon in coal, in graphite, and so on, also lives within human beings as a metamorphosed substance; that on the one side it acts only in death-bringing compounds and on the other only in compounds of resurrection; if one speaks not only of the metamorphoses of carbon, which in the various stages of the earth's evolution produced diamond, coal, and graphite; if one realizes that there are different kinds of metamorphosis of carbon in the human being that can become inwardly alive, can be spiritualized, can mediate between death and life; if one understands this, one has in this understanding an immediate source of inspiration. If you can understand this, you will find the right approach to teaching in school; it is essential for the right approach to occur to you; you should not stand in the classroom with such a sour look that anyone can tell from your expression that you stand before the children in a morose, surly mood. Such a mood is impossible if you possess inwardly mobile, creative knowledge. Then, in all humility, you will realize the importance of the work, and this will reveal itself even in your facial expression while teaching. Your expression is then naturally illuminated by the etheric and astral and unites with outer form to create a whole.

A teacher's face has three main nuances of expression, with any number of intermediate stages. There is the face with which teachers meet an ordinary person, when they forget that they are teachers and simply engage in natural conversation. There is the face teachers have when they have finished their lesson and leave the classroom; and there is the face they have in the classroom. We may often be ashamed of human nature when we see the difference in the teachers' faces when they are going into their classroom and when they leave it. These things are connected with the whole consciousness of the teacher. Perhaps it may comfort you a little if I say that under the influence of an active, vital knowledge every face becomes twice as beautiful as it is otherwise, but the knowledge must do its work, the knowledge must live, and teachers' faces should always be alive, inwardly expressive, especially when they are giving lessons. The importance in what I'm telling you is not that you should know these things, but that they should work on your life of feeling [*Gemüt*], strengthening you, giving you the vigor to spiritualize your profession.

Teachers ought to be conscious, especially nowadays, of their great social task, and they should ponder this task a great deal. The teacher, above all others, should be deeply permeated with awareness of the great needs of modern civilization.

I will give you an example of what is needed in order to adopt the right attitude in our civilization today. You have all heard of Mahatma Gandhi who, since the war, or really since 1914, has set a movement going for the liberation of India from English rule. Gandhi's activities began first in South Africa with the aim of helping the Indians who were living there under appalling conditions, and for whose emancipation he did a great deal before 1914. Then he went to India itself and instituted a movement for liberation there. I shall speak today only of what took place when the final verdict was passed on Mahatma Gandhi, and omit the court proceedings leading up to it. I would like to speak only of the last act in the drama, as it were, that took place between him and his judge. Gandhi had been accused of stirring up the Indian people against British rule in order to make India independent. Being a lawyer, he conducted his own defense and had not the slightest doubt that he would be condemned. In his speech—I cannot quote the actual words—he spoke more or less to the following effect, "My Lords, I beg of you to condemn me in accordance with the full strength of the law. I am perfectly aware that in the eyes of British law in India my crime is the gravest one imaginable. I do not plead any mitigating circumstances; I beg of you to condemn me with the full strength of the law. I affirm, moreover, that my condemnation is required not only in obedience to the principles of outer justice but to the principles of expediency of the British government. For if I were to be acquitted I should feel it incumbent upon me to continue to propagate the movement, and millions of Indians would join it. My acquittal would lead to results that I regard as my duty."

The contents of this speech are very characteristic of what lives and weaves in our time. Gandhi says he must of necessity be condemned, and declares it his duty to continue the activity for which he is to be condemned. The judge replied, "Mahatma Gandhi, you have rendered my task of sentencing you immeasurably easier, because you have made it clear that I must of necessity condemn you. It is obvious that you have transgressed against British law, but you and all those present will realize how hard it will be for me to sentence you. It is clear that a large portion of the Indian people looks upon you as a saint, as one who has taken up his task in obedience to the highest duties devolving upon humanity. The judgment I shall pass on you will be looked upon by the majority of the Indian people as the condemnation of a human being who has devoted himself to the highest service of humanity. Clearly, however, British law must in all severity be put into effect against you. You would regard it as your duty, if you were acquitted, to continue tomorrow what you were doing yesterday. We on our side have to regard it as our most solemn duty to make that impossible. I condemn you in the full consciousness that my sentence will in turn be condemned by millions. I condemn you while admiring your actions, but condemn you I must." Gandhi's sentence was six years at hard labor.

You could hardly find a more striking example of what is characteristic of our times. We have two levels of actuality before us. Below is the level of truth, the level where the accused declares that if he is acquitted, it will be his solemn duty to continue what he must define as criminal in face of outer law. On the level of truth, also, we have the judge's statement that he admires the one whom, out of duty to his government, he sentences to six years' hard labor. Above, at the level of facts, you have what the accused in this case, because he is a great soul, defined as crime: the crime that is his duty and that he would at once continue were he to be acquitted. Whereas on the one level you have the admiration of the judge for a great human being, on the other you have the passing of judgment and its outer justification. You have truths below, facts above, which have nothing to do with one another. They touch on one another at only one point, at the point where they confront each other in statement and counterstatement.

Here, my dear friends, you have a most striking example of the fact that nowadays we have a level of truth and a level of untruth. The level of untruth, however, is in public events, and at no point are the two levels in touch with each other. We must keep this clearly in mind, because it is intimately bound up with the whole life of spirit of our times. An example as striking as this reveals things that occur everywhere but are usually less obvious and startling. We must achieve first, however, a real consciousness of what has come to pass in the present in order to put truth in the place of what is happening in the present. We simply must find the true path. Naturally, it is not a matter of overturning everything or of engaging in false radicalism, which leads only to destruction, but of seeing what one can do. We have to find the way to a clear insight and then work in the area where our efforts can be most fruitful.

The most fruitful sphere of activity is education. There, even if education is controlled by dictatorial rules and standards, teachers can let what they gain from a true feeling for their profession flow into their lessons. They must, however, have a knowledge of the human being that will imbue life and spirit into what is otherwise dead knowledge, and, on the other hand, have an enthusiasm arising from a really free and open-minded conception of what life today actually is. You must be clear that in outer life you are at the level above, but as a teacher facing children it is possible to maintain the level below. It is not by practicing an educational method based on clichés, but by acquiring real enthusiasm for your profession, the consciousness of your profession, that you can emancipate yourselves from the constraints in educational activity and be inspired by the majesty contained in a true knowledge of humanity. It is sometimes a very bitter experience to speak to anthroposophists, for example, and be compelled to say things that turn what people have learned upside down (though not in a bad sense)—and then to find that no attention is paid to what has been said. If you grasped the full weight of what I said in the lecture yesterday[12] about meteoric iron, for instance, you might well be astonished at the indifference with which such a matter is received. I can understand this in the case of people who have not learned anything, but in the case of those who are conversant with the scientific concepts about iron, it is incomprehensible. But the world is like that today.

---

12. Rudolf Steiner, "The Michael Inspiration, Spiritual Milestones in the Course of the Year," *The Festivals and Their Meaning*, London, Rudolf Steiner Press, 1996.

That is not, however, how the world *should* be in the head, and especially in the heart, of teachers and educators. They must be filled with the consciousness that all the knowledge acquired through modern science is dead knowledge out of which we must create something living, and the only sort of knowledge that we can use in school arises from this enthusiasm. If you are permeated on the one hand with the enthusiasm kindled by such a knowledge of the human being, and on the other with the consciousness of the necessity to put truth in place of the lies that are accepted today—you can find no more impressive example than the legal case I just described to you—if you realize this necessity with your whole being and know that it is the teacher's task to find the right direction through recognition of this necessity, and in face of the appalling crudities inherent in what appears to be truth in public life today, then something happens within the human being that colors every sphere. You will become a different kind of eurythmy teacher, a different kind of art teacher, a different kind of mathematics teacher. In every sphere you will become different if you are permeated in the real sense by this consciousness. Everything is established by this enthusiasm. This is not the time to talk about the niceties of this or that method. We must bring life into the world, which through its dead intellectualism is faced with the danger of falling still further into death.

Basically, we have fallen out of the habit of being inwardly incensed by things as they are. If you merely pull a long face, however, about things that ought to be rejected in our civilization, you certainly will not be able to educate. That is why it is so necessary from time to time to speak of things in such a way that they can really take hold of our feeling [*Gemüt*]. If you go away from these lectures with nothing more than the feeling that there has to be a change in the spiritual factors governing the world today, then you will have grasped my aim in giving them.

The dragon takes on the most diverse forms; takes on every possible form. Those that arise from human emotions are harmful enough, but not nearly as harmful as the form the dragon acquires from the dead and deadening knowledge that prevails today. There the dragon becomes especially horrible. One might almost say that the correct symbol for institutions of higher education today would be a thick, black pall hung somewhere on the wall of every lecture room. Then one would realize that behind it is something that must not be shown, because to do so would throw a strange light on what goes on in these lecture rooms! Behind the black pall there should be a picture of Michael's battle with the dragon, the battle with deadening intellectualism. What I have said today shows you how the struggle between Michael and the dragon should live in teachers. What I wanted to present to you is this: we must become aware of Michael's battle; it must become a reality for us if we are to celebrate Michaelmas in the right way. No one is more called upon to play a part in inaugurating the Michael festival in the right way than the teacher. Teachers should unite themselves with Michael in a particularly close way, for to live in these times means simply to crawl into the dragon and further the old intellectual operation. To live in the truth means to unite oneself with Michael. We must unite ourselves with Michael whenever we enter the classroom; only through this can we bring with us the necessary strength. Verily, Michael is strong! If we understand Michael's struggle with the dragon in a particular sphere, we are working for the healing of humanity in the future. If I had been asked to give these lectures a title, I would have had to say: Michael's Struggle with the Dragon, Presented for the Teachers at the Waldorf School. One should not speak about the possibility of celebrating a Michael festival now, but rather give thought to introducing into the most diverse spheres of life the kind of consciousness with which a Michael festival could be connected. If you can make these things come alive in your hearts, can permeate your souls with them; if you can bring this consciousness with you into the classroom and sustain it there in complete tranquility, without any element of agitation or high-sounding phrases; if you can let yourselves be inspired to unpretentious action through what can be kindled in your consciousness by surrender to these necessities, then you will enter into the alliance with Michael, as is essential for the teacher and educator.

THE FOUNDATIONS
OF WALDORF EDUCATION

The First Free Waldorf School opened its doors in Stuttgart, Germany, in September, 1919, under the auspices of Emil Molt, the Director of the Waldorf Astoria Cigarette Company and a student of Rudolf Steiner's spiritual science and particularly of Steiner's call for social renewal.

It was only the previous year—amid the social chaos following the end of World War I—that Emil Molt, responding to Steiner's prognosis that truly human change would not be possible unless a sufficient number of people received an education that developed the whole human being, decided to create a school for his workers' children. Conversations with the minister of education and with Rudolf Steiner, in early 1919, then led rapidly to the forming of the first school.

Since that time, more than 900 schools have opened around the globe—from Italy, France, Portugal, Spain, Holland, Belgium, Great Britain, Norway, Finland, and Sweden to Russia, Georgia, Poland, Hungary, Romania, Israel, Africa, Australia, Brazil, Chile, Peru, Argentina, Japan, China, and others—making the Waldorf school movement the largest independent school movement in the world. The United States, Canada, and Mexico alone now have around 200 schools.

Although each Waldorf school is independent, and although there is a healthy oral tradition going back to the first Waldorf teachers and to Steiner himself, as well as a growing body of secondary literature, the true foundations of the Waldorf approach and spirit remain the many lectures that Rudolf Steiner gave on the subject. For five years (1919–24), Rudolf Steiner, while simultaneously working on many other fronts, tirelessly dedicated himself to the dissemination of the idea of Waldorf education. He gave manifold lectures to teachers, parents, the general public, and even the children themselves. New schools were founded. The movement grew.

While many of Steiner's foundational lectures have been translated and published in the past, some have never appeared in English, and many have been virtually unobtainable for years. To remedy this situation and to establish a coherent basis for Waldorf education, Anthroposophic Press has decided to publish the complete series of Steiner lectures and writings on education in a uniform series. This series will thus constitute an authoritative foundation for work in educational renewal, for Waldorf teachers, parents, and educators generally.

RUDOLF STEINER'S LECTURES
AND WRITINGS ON EDUCATION

I. *Allgemeine Menschenkunde als Grundlage der Pädagogik. Pädagogischer Grundkurs*, 14 Lectures, Stuttgart, 1919 (GA 293). Previously *Study of Man*. **The Foundations of Human Experience** (Anthroposophic Press, 1996).

II. *Erziehungskunst Methodische-Didaktisches*, 14 Lectures, Stuttgart, 1919 (GA 294). **Practical Advice to Teachers** (Rudolf Steiner Press, 1988).

III. *Erziehungskunst Methodische-Didaktisches*, 15 Discussions, Stuttgart, 1919 (GA 295). **Discussions with Teachers** (Anthroposophic Press, 1997).

IV. *Die Erziehungsfrage als soziale Frage*, 6 Lectures, Dornach, 1919 (GA 296). **Education as a Force for Social Change** (previously *Education as a Social Problem*) (Anthroposophic Press, 1997).

V. *Die Waldorf Schule und ihr Geist*, 6 Lectures, Stuttgart and Basel, 1919 (GA 297). **The Spirit of the Waldorf School** (Anthroposophic Press, 1995).

VI. *Rudolf Steiner in der Waldorfschule, Vorträge und Ansprachen*, Stuttgart, 1919–1924 (GA 298). **Rudolf Steiner in the Waldorf School: Lectures and Conversations** (Anthroposophic Press, 1996).

VII. *Geisteswissenschaftliche Sprachbetrachtungen*, 6 Lectures, Stuttgart, 1919 (GA 299). **The Genius of Language** (Anthroposophic Press, 1995).

VIII. *Konferenzen mit den Lehren der Freien Waldorfschule 1919–1924*, 3 Volumes (GA 300). **Faculty Meetings with Rudolf Steiner**, 2 volumes (Anthroposophic Press, 1998).

IX. *Die Erneuerung der Pädagogisch-didaktischen Kunst durch Geisteswissenschaft*, 14 Lectures, Basel, 1920 (GA 301). **The Renewal of Education** (Anthroposophic Press, 2001).

X. *Menschenerkenntnis und Unterrichtsgestaltung*, 8 Lectures, Stuttgart, 1921 (GA 302). Previously *The Supplementary Course—Upper School* and *Waldorf Education for Adolescence*) **Education for Adolescents** (Anthroposophic Press, 1996).

XI. *Erziehung und Unterricht aus Menschenerkenntnis*, 7 Lectures, Stuttgart, 1920, 1922, 1923 (GA 302a). **Balance in Teaching** (Anthroposophic Press, 2007).

XII. *Die Gesunder Entwicklung des Menschenwesens*, 16 Lectures, Dornach, 1921–22 (GA 303). **Soul Economy: Body, Soul, and Spirit in Waldorf Education** (Anthroposophic Press, 2003).

XIII. *Erziehungs- und Unterrichtsmethoden auf Anthroposophischer Grundlage*, 9 Public Lectures, various cities, 1921–22 (GA 304). **Waldorf Education and Anthroposophy 1** (Anthroposophic Press, 1995).

XIV. *Anthroposophische Menschenkunde und Pädagogik,* 9 Public Lectures, various cities, 1923–24 (GA 304a). **Waldorf Education and Anthroposophy 2** (Anthroposophic Press, 1996).

XV. *Die geistig-seelischen Grundkräfte der Erziehungskunst,* 12 Lectures, 1 Special Lecture, Oxford 1922 (GA 305). **The Spiritual Ground of Education** (Anthroposophic Press, 2004).

XVI. *Die pädagogische Praxis vom Gesichtspunkte geisteswissenschaftlicher Menschenerkenntnis,* 8 Lectures, Dornach, 1923 (GA 306). **The Child's Changing Consciousness As the Basis of Pedagogical Practice** (Anthroposophic Press, 1996).

XVII. *Gegenwärtiges Geistesleben und Erziehung,* 4 Lectures, Ilkeley, 1923 (GA 307). **A Modern Art of Education** (Anthroposophic Press, 2004) and **Education and Modern Spiritual Life** (Garber Publications, 1989).

XVIII. *Die Methodik des Lehrens und die Lebensbedingungen des Erziehens,* 5 Lectures, Stuttgart, 1924 (GA 308). **The Essentials of Education** (Anthroposophic Press, 1997).

XIX. *Anthroposophische Pädagogik und ihre Voraussetzungen,* 5 Lectures, Bern, 1924 (GA 309). **The Roots of Education** (Anthroposophic Press, 1997).

XX. *Der pädagogische Wert der Menschenerkenntnis und der Kulturwert der Pädagogik,* 10 Public Lectures, Arnheim, 1924 (GA 310). **Human Values in Education** (Rudolf Steiner Press, 1971).

XXI. *Die Kunst des Erziehens aus dem Erfassen der Menschenwesenheit,* 7 Lectures, Torquay, 1924 (GA 311). **The Kingdom of Childhood** (Anthroposophic Press, 1995).

XXII. *Geisteswissenschaftliche Impulse zur Entwicklung der Physik. Erster naturwissenschaftliche Kurs: Licht, Farbe, Ton—Masse, Elektrizität, Magnetismus,* 10 Lectures, Stuttgart, 1919–20 (GA 320). **The Light Course** (Anthroposophic Press, 2001).

XXIII. *Geisteswissenschaftliche Impulse zur Entwicklung der Physik. Zweiter naturwissenschaftliche Kurs: die Wärme auf der Grenze positiver und negativer Materialität,* 14 Lectures, Stuttgart, 1920 (GA 321). **The Warmth Course** (Mercury Press, 1988).

XXIV. *Das Verhältnis der verschiedenen naturwissenschaftlichen Gebiete zur Astronomie. Dritter naturwissenschaftliche Kurs: Himmelskunde in Beziehung zum Menschen und zur Menschenkunde,* 18 Lectures, Stuttgart, 1921 (GA 323). Available in typescript only as *"The Relation of the Diverse Branches of Natural Science to Astronomy."*

XXV. **The Education of the Child and Early Lectures on Education** (A collection) (Anthroposophic Press, 1996).

XXVI. Miscellaneous.

INDEX

During the last two decades of the nineteenth century the Austrian-born Rudolf Steiner (1861–1925) became a respected and well-published scientific, literary, and philosophical scholar, particularly known for his work on Goethe's scientific writings. After the turn of the century he began to develop his earlier philosophical principles into an approach to methodical research of psychological and spiritual phenomena.

His multifaceted genius has led to innovative and holistic approaches in medicine, philosophy, religion, education (Waldorf schools), special education, economics, agriculture (Biodynamic method), science, architecture, drama, the new arts of speech and eurythmy, and other fields of activity. In 1924 he founded the General Anthroposophical Society, which today has branches throughout the world.

CPSIA information can be obtained at www.ICGtesting.com
Printed in the USA
LVOW13s0746080414

380778LV00001B/29/P